Running in Place

Running
in Place

✴ ✴

HOW BILL CLINTON
DISAPPOINTED AMERICA

Richard Reeves

Andrews and McMeel

A UNIVERSAL PRESS SYNDICATE COMPANY

Kansas City

Library of Congress Cataloging-in-Publication Data

Reeves, Richard.
    Running in place : how Bill Clinton disappointed America / by
Richard Reeves.
        p. cm.
    ISBN 0–8362–1091–3 (pbk.)
    1. United States—Politics and government—1993–   2. Clin-
ton, Bill, 1946–   . I. Title.
    E885.R44   1996
    973.929—dc20   95–46984
                                                              CIP

*This book is for
Ian Howard Fyfe,
first grandchild*

Contents

Foreword   ix

1. Politics by the Numbers   3

2. A Tale of Two Congresses   13

3. Bill Clinton, Bothered and Bewildered   19

4. Passion for Distinction   39

5. Smart and Smarter and Too Smart   49

6. Lifestyles of Rich and Famous
    Correspondents   53

7. Clinton the Murderer!   71

8. Prolonged Adolescence   79

9. The Kids in the White House   83

10. HRC: The First Lady   91

11. Sex and the Clinton Collapse   99

12. Somebody up There Doesn't Like Me   105

Foreword

In writing books about four presidents—John F. Kennedy, Gerald Ford, Jimmy Carter, and Ronald Reagan—I have learned one big thing: The presidency of the United States, the job itself, is sui generis. Only forty-two men, from George Washington to William Jefferson Clinton, truly know what it is like to be president. One of them, Kennedy, said this to a historian in 1962: "No one has a right to grade a President—not even poor James Buchanan—who has not sat in his chair, examined the mail and information that came across his desk, and learned why he made his decisions."

I agree with that, at least in the abstract. But I know, too, that the rest of us, historians or ordinary citizens, are probably as qualified to judge as presidents are to serve. There is no adequate preparation for the presidency and perhaps there never has been. The presidency is an act of faith, the rather touching democratic belief that one among the many is capable of winning the consent of the rest to lead or guide us through times and events that are dangerous and divisive. The many, of course, do not always want leadership, particularly when times are good (for them)—and are suspicious of leadership even when there is consensus that it is necessary. Independence, or individualism, and that certain mistrust of power exercised by others are at the heart of being American.

Bill Clinton, a seventeen-year-old high school senior from Hot Springs, Arkansas, a member of his state's delegation to Boys Nation, was among hundreds of students from everywhere in the country invited to the White House on July 24, 1963. He shook hands with President Kennedy that day and there is a photograph to prove it. Photo in hand, Clinton has said many times that the brief encounter had inspired him to make politics his life.

Kennedy was and is rightly an inspiration to any young man or woman yearning to reach a high place. The thirty-fifth president had many advantages, particularly family wealth, but the presidency is a little too big to buy. Jack Kennedy was a young man in a hurry, and he was not willing to wait his turn. He directly challenged the institution he wanted to control, the political system. After him, no one else wanted to wait either, and few institutions were rigid enough or flexible enough to survive impatient, ambition-driven challenges. When Kennedy, a forty-three-year-old junior member of the Senate, was asked early in 1960 why he thought he should be president, he answered: "I look around me at the others in the race, and I say to myself, well, if they think they can do it, why not me?" *Why not me?* "That's the answer. And I think it's enough. . . . This is the time for me."

And 1992 was the time for Bill Clinton. Others whose candidacies were seen as more compelling—Mario Cuomo, Bill Bradley, and Sam Nunn among them—were waiting for a better moment. Asked if he wanted to be president, Senator Bradley said, "Yes, sometime." But people who say "sometime" are not in the running or eligible for the winning. Presidents since Kennedy—with the exception of Ford, who was never elected to the job—have been self-selected and self-created.

There could not have been a less likely future president than the young man who shook Kennedy's hand. His rise was almost an American equivalent of finding a Dalai Lama—a poor boy from the backwoods. Of course, holy men seek out a baby in Tibet and it is the other way around with us, the baby who wants to be president seeks out the credentials and celebrity and people who can help him in his quest.

Though Kennedy and Clinton were quite different in many ways, there were words I wrote about one that I would write about the other: "He was a gifted professional politician reacting to events he often neither foresaw nor understood, handling some well, others badly, but always ready with plausible explanations. He was intelligent, detached, curious, candid if not always honest, careless and dangerously disorganized. He was very impatient, addicted to excitement, living his life as if it were a race against boredom. He was a man of soaring charm in a business that magnifies and institutionalizes personal seduction. He believed that one-on-one he would always prevail—a notion that betrayed him . . .

"He was decisive, but never made a decision until he had to, and then invariably chose the most moderate of available options," I wrote of John Kennedy. Those words are from my book *President Kennedy: Profile of Power* published in October of 1993. President Clinton, whom I had occasionally covered as a reporter, invited me to the White House then and we talked for a couple of hours, mostly about Kennedy. Among the things he asked was this: "How could Kennedy keep decisions open for so long?"

The answer was that Kennedy did not think out loud or in public. President Clinton did, and paid a high price, convincing many millions of Americans that he was hopelessly indecisive, confused and unsure. "Flip-flopping" is the term of political art.

In fact, Bill Clinton has been a relatively effective president in relatively difficult times. In his first year, he pushed legislation through a Democratic Congress at speed that almost matched the glory days of Lyndon Johnson. Unemployment and inflation have decreased on his watch and his first two budgets reduced the rate of federal deficit spending from five percent of the gross domestic product at the end of the Reagan-George Bush years to 2.5 percent—quite an achievement for a president reflexively attacked as a big-spending liberal. He

has certainly been unsure on foreign policy, but the results have not been all that bad. The nation is not at war,
there has been some success in disarming the nuclear-
ready states of the former Soviet Union, and the United
States has diplomatically supplanted the United Nations
as the world's peacemaker of last resort. And, although
almost anything seems possible when a microphone is
near, Clinton has made some stirring speeches, most
notably on racial hostility, which has always been the
country's most critical threat to domestic tranquility.

By the end of his third year as president, Clinton's
own domestic tranquility became critical for the second
or third time when his wife, Hillary Rodham Clinton, became the focus of investigations of small scandals involv-
ing suspicious land dealings in Arkansas and the impet-
uous firing of a few career White House employees.
While congressional Republicans accused her of obstruct-
ing justice in the disappearance and re-discovery of legal
documents, one of their journalistic allies, William Safire of the *New York Times,* was more blunt, calling her
"a congenital liar." Inside the White House, many of the
president's men considered their boss a hostage to his
wife and her many moods. In simplified analysis, the
cycles of President Clinton's tenure—up the first year,
down the second, up again in the third year and then
down at the beginning of the campaign year, 1996—seemed
to have less to do with events in the world than with what
went on upstairs in the family quarters of the White House.

By then, Clinton seemed to have lost the confidence of half the nation—and that divide looked permanent. He no longer has the initiative that is a president's right and has allowed his adversaries to move the mainstream on the gut issues of welfare, health care, education, regulation, taxation and even the role of government itself. Many members of his own party, the Democrats, sputtering of betrayal, wondered whether they were present at the dismantling of the party's patrimony, the New Deal of Franklin D. Roosevelt.

As he officially began his campaign for re-election, there was no question that Bill Clinton was still the best politician of his generation. He had managed to confuse his enemies by giving in to the wild-eyed Republicans of the 104th Congress as often as he opposed them. Perhaps more important, by acting more assertively on foreign policy and staying off television unless he had something to say, he was beginning to look presidential and act like *the* president. Disappointed Democratic friends were dropping out of politics, going home rather than deal with the new Washington, and the Republicans brought forth a pretty motley crew of 1996 candidates. President Clinton could be re-elected and he had obviously learned to govern, but it seemed to be too late. He had almost certainly lost his chance to be an agent of change and lead a great nation. Many note and long remember one of the great lines by the sixteenth president, Abraham Lincoln, the one warning that you can't fool all the people all of the time. But what Lincoln said just before that is rarely quoted. It may define the greatest problem of the forty-second president, Bill Clinton: "If you once forfeit the confidence of your fellow citizens, you can never regain their respect and esteem."

Richard Reeves
Pacific Palisades, California

January 1996

Running in Place

1.
Politics by the Numbers

Being president of the United States has not always been as much fun as William Jefferson Clinton thought it would be in all the years he tried to figure out how to get the job. He had been in the White House almost two years when I asked him why he felt he had to be on television so much. He did not much like the question.

"The inference there is wrong—that I want to be on television every night," he said. The press made him do it. "Because President Reagan was shot, the press takes the position that they have an absolute right to be with me wherever I am spending the night, which means they want a picture of me running every day, which I think is wrong and bad and overexposes the president."

"Why can't you stop that?" I asked.

"Ask him," he said, nodding toward Mark Gearan, his communications director at the time, who was sitting across from me on one of the couches in the Oval Office of the White House.

"You have to live in a prison," Clinton continued. "Let

me give you an example. I went to western Pennsylvania recently, and we had ten thousand people in a little town called—what was that called? Anyway, it was wonderful . . . for a health care rally. And I was fascinated because on the way in, it was two whole miles of nothing but auto body shops, muffler shops, auto repair shops, and car dealerships. I've never seen anything like it. And all these guys were out there, you know, not exactly my constituency.

"At any other time I would have stopped and had a visit with those people. You know, I couldn't stop and have a visit with those people because the entire press corps would have stopped, and if they could have gotten two people to say something bad, then that might have been the story on television that night instead of going there to talk to ten thousand.

"So I had to sit there like Buddha in chains."

He came back to it again, saying: "I would have really enjoyed talking to those guys at those places, and it would have helped me stay, I mean, in better touch with how they feel; it would have helped me a lot. But if my goal as president is to communicate with the American people, I would have run a very high risk that the message I wanted to send out to the people that night wouldn't get there."

It was hard for me to tell right then, in October of 1994, whether he was madder at me for asking the question or at the job or the press or the people. Maybe he was mad

4

at Gearan or the thousand or so men and women in the Executive Office of the President who are collectively called "The White House" and whose principal responsibility was to keep Clinton "on message"—a term from the advertising business which means sticking to the script. They were all supposed to make sure that Clinton said only what he was supposed to say on a given day. No matter how smart a president is these days—and Clinton is very smart—each day begins with meetings to decide the message. Words, often poll-tested, are worked out in advance to have a specified effect on the consumers (or voters) of America. And Bill Clinton, who loves to talk, loves to think out loud and wander all over the place, was famous for going "off message" if he slipped the chains of office and staff.

A couple of weeks after that conversation, it was clear that the president was indeed mad at the people, at least some of the people who had voted against his party, the Democrats, in the midterm elections on November 8, 1994. Like many a politician after a losing election, he blamed the people. After all he wanted to do for them and tried to do for them—this!

Usually candidates keep such thoughts to themselves, a most notable exception being Richard Tuck, a political operative in the employ of Kennedy campaigns, who as a young man ran for a state assembly seat in Los Angeles in the 1960s. He lost the race and offered a six-word concession speech: "The people have spoken—the bastards!" That is what Clinton meant, too, though he tried to clean up the thought. At a Democratic Leadership Council dinner in Washington after the 1994 elections, he deviated from a text he had written himself to say: "The very people you try hardest to help are those who turn away. . . . The people who are working harder for lower wages and less security than they were ten years ago, they're the people I ran to help."

Right. He did the same thing, blaming the people for his own failings, almost a year later. On *Air Force One* at the end of September 1995, jetting home after a week of fund-raising around the country for his 1996 reelection campaign, the president, in blue jeans and cowboy boots, came back to talk to reporters for forty-five minutes, saying at one point: "What makes people insecure is when they feel they're lost in the fun house. They're in a room where something can hit them from any direction at any time. . . . I'm also trying to get people out of their funk."

A week later, he told a fund-raising dinner in Houston, Texas, that he had raised taxes "too much" in 1993—sort of blaming the 103rd Congress, the Democratic one, for making him do it. Two weeks after that, in a telephone call to a syndicated columnist, Ben Wattenberg, he said he was against the welfare reform plan he had submitted to the Democrats. If there was a pattern to such backing-and-filling, it was this: Most of Bill Clinton's speeches and statements were reactive, often defensive and usually about himself—explaining himself past, present or future, rather than mobilizing, educating or inspiring the people of the country. He did not make much use of the "bully pulpit" as Theodore Roosevelt called the office—this one sometimes seemed more puppy pulpit.

Clinton's public postelection funk was a small thing compared with his private eruptions—the man uses his young staff as shock absorbers on bad days. He was upset at what pollsters and analysts concluded was a significant defection of white working men—"the people I ran to help"—from the Democratic Party. Their grandfathers and fathers had been devoted to the Democratic Party in the days of Franklin Delano Roosevelt and John F. Kennedy, but many of them voted for Republicans this day. The Republicans had been a minority in the 103rd Congress but they had harassed and checked the Democratic leadership and the Democratic president in the final months of that session, the run-up to the 1994 elections. In the Senate, the disciplined Republican minority, led by Senator Robert Dole, blocked Clinton legislation with twenty filibusters in two months, more than had been used in the previous twenty years.

"They reinforced the image that the federal government doesn't work," Clinton said to me with real bitterness. "So if they throw a wrench in the works, instead of being punished for throwing the wrench, they actually in a perverse way get rewarded. I think that's been their theory all along."

If so, it worked. The elections of November 8, 1994

gave the Republicans control of both the Senate and the House of Representatives for the first time in forty-eight years in the 104th Congress, which convened on New Year's Day of 1995.

*   *

By late January, the president had settled down and accepted the election results. That is what he most believes in, the numbers—votes. And polls, too. In October of 1993, he and I had talked about whether or not United States troops should be used to reinstate the exiled president of Haiti, Jean Bertrand Aristide. Clinton met questions about the Haitian's legitimacy and reports that he was not exactly the most stable of men—a little nuts, actually, said the Central Intelligence Agency—with a defining politician's answer: "I know what they say about him, but he got 67 percent of the vote."

Votes are the moral imperative of Bill Clinton's business. The true qualification for public office is winning it.

So, with the Republicans, too, Clinton bowed to the higher authority of electoral numbers. For a few weeks he rallied Democrats in Congress to take on the new Republican majorities. His Democrats zigged his way, a little reluctantly some of them, ready to follow their chief into this new fight. And then he zagged. On January 24, 1995, Clinton began his third State of the Union Address by honoring the winners: "Our democracy has spoken . . . " Then he surrendered to enemies who were taking no prisoners.

The people had spoken. "Good people of good will want us to find common ground," he said later. If there was such ground, it would be a an odd-sized piece of political turf, accommodating burning-eyed Republican conservatives who believed in something and did not want to know anything else, and the flap-tongued Democratic president who seemed to know everything and believe in nothing. The new Republicans were intent on repairing a country they believed had been crippled and corrupted by the New Deal, the New Frontier, and the Great Society—in other words, they wanted to grind the Democrats and their proudest works into dust.

Reaching out, Clinton could not even understand the language of the victors. He said it had always been his goal to "put" money in the pockets of what he called "mainstream" Americans. What conservatives say is that they want the government to "leave" money in the pockets of "taxpayers." Those are the people the new Republican Speaker of the House, Newt Gingrich, called "normal" Americans, specifically saying he meant normal compared with Bill and Hillary Clinton.

*   *

It would be a mistake to ever write off Bill Clinton as a politician. Said one of his young men, Rahm Emanuel, the White House political director: "There is no one in politics who can touch Bill Clinton when he's feeling good and on message." Clinton saw himself giving the Republicans of the 104th Congress enough rope to hang themselves, which also happened to be enough for them to strangle him—or at least tie him up. He was willing to take that chance—the best of his options, he thought. He was willing and able to say whatever had to be said, even words that most of his forty-one predecessors would have choked on: "The Constitution gives me relevance. . . . The president is relevant here . . . "

Yes, presidents choose. Presidents can set or move a national agenda. They can lead. Or they can just try to survive. Bill Clinton prefers survival—that is his business, too. Clinton had even found the appropriate Abraham Lincoln maxim to explain the fact that he was not only accepting the results, he was ready for catch-up and cohabitation. In an interview after the election, Clinton quoted the sixteenth president as saying, "I am controlled by events. My policy is to have no policy." The words were not quite right, but the thought was. Lincoln was a professional, too, and he reflected the reactive nature of politicians in a letter to a friend in 1864: "I claim not to have controlled events, but confess plainly that events have controlled me." In Clinton's case, he followed that paraphrase by adding: "I think this is a time when we have to be highly flexible. We have to be willing to admit it when we make a mistake and change course."

The forty-second president is a compleat democrat, ever ready to change course to tack with the opinion of the great American public—as it drifts or lurches one way or another. Bill Clinton could be called the first true president of a new American public opinion democracy, acting as a facilitator for the wobbly will of the people. He accepted a 2 percent shift in the overall congressional vote as the marching orders for the last two years of his term. The new Republican leaders of Congress smirked and whispered to each other like schoolboys as the president spoke favorably of the "Contract with America," the ten-point conservative campaign plan to tear down the governmental structure erected by Democratic presidents. By Clinton's reckoning, the speech worked. He accepted relatively favorable poll numbers after the message as numerical validation that he had said the right words for the moment.

That long State of the Union message on January 24, one hour and twenty minutes, was a surprise to almost everyone—not only to the Democrats in Congress who expected the leader of their party to challenge the Republicans, but also to the leader's own staff as well. Only three hours before the television lights went on, the White House chief of staff, Leon Panetta, had told selected reporters—on "background," meaning reporters could use the information but not identify the source— that the speech would be forty minutes long and the greatest emphasis would be on programs to discourage teenage pregnancy. Obviously he did not know that the president and Hillary Rodham Clinton were at that moment working alone together, adding forty more minutes of material but eliminating the pregnancy section.

The last-minute changes actually should not have been a shock in the Clinton White House, where every one of the thousand staff members seemed to have the power to say "No" but only two people, the president and his wife, had the power to say "Yes."

2.
A Tale of
Two Congresses

The 1995 State of the Union message neatly divided President Clinton's term into two parts with a single reality: He reacted to the numbers of the day. On the night of January 24, 1995, he accepted the Republicans' claim of a mandate in the 104th Congress and pledged to work with them. More than two years before he had accepted the primacy of the Democratic 103rd Congress and made the same pledge to Democratic leaders. The agendas of the two Congresses were diametrically opposed, but Clinton went with the numbers. The people had spoken, and whether or not they knew what they were talking about, the president was not about to argue with them.

It was on November 15, 1992, seven days after he defeated president George Bush—winning 43 percent of the vote in a three-man field—that the president-elect met with the congressional leadership at his home in Arkansas, the governor's mansion in Little Rock. Over roast beef and cheese potatoes, he was bombarded by tales of how President Jimmy Carter, another southern governor, had failed as president in the late 1970s because he confronted Congress. The message was: You, sir, will succeed if you become our friend.

As Clinton talked with the men from Washington, Harry Thomason, the producer of *Designing Women* and other television winners, walked into the building of a failed local newspaper, the *Arkansas Gazette,* which was being used as transition headquarters. The producer, who had known Bill and Hillary Clinton for years, was with Al From, the founder of the Democratic Leadership Council, so-called "New Democrats" (read conservative Democrats) Clinton sometimes claimed as political kin when it suited his purposes. The halls were clogged with Washingtonians who had come south in attendance to House Speaker Thomas Foley and his sidekick, Majority Leader Richard Gephardt, and Senate Majority Leader George Mitchell. "Who are all these people?" asked Thomason.

From answered: "These are the people who tried to beat us."

The next morning the president-elect was outside the governor's mansion at a press conference with his new friends from Washington, telling reporters: "Pennsylvania Avenue will run both ways again. . . . I don't want a continuation of the Cold War between Congress and the White House."

"Partnership . . . cooperation . . . teamwork," the president-elect said at that press conference. At dinner with the older Democrats, he had backed away from commitments to force a cutback in the size of congressional staffs and to fight for a presidential line-item veto power over legislation. On the morning after, he stood up to be counted with the leaders of the second-most-disliked institution in the country, old-time Democrats who had more title than power. Congressional approval rates stood at about 30 percent, better only than the press's 20 percent or so. The men he stood with were significantly more liberal than members they were supposed to lead, who were, in turn, more liberal than the people who had voted for Clinton the week before, to say nothing of the 57 percent of American voters who had cast their ballots for President George Bush or Ross Perot.

Somehow, Cinton, who had run calling himself "the agent of change," did not understand that—or did not understand what he was signing up for with the party's agents of the status quo. It was as if he had tied a boulder to his ankle and sat in the back of the boat of state, letting Foley and Mitchell row. That crew produced some significant successes at first, but the boat tipped over in the second year of Clinton's presidency. The conventional wisdom on November 9, 1994, the day after the midterm elections, was that President Clinton had brought down the Democrats of Congress. But the opposite was more true. Only late in the 1994 midterm campaign did he finally understand what had happened, turning to an aide and saying, "I've lashed myself to Congress like Ahab and Moby Dick."

In Little Rock that night in 1992, the president-elect, whether he knew it or not, signed on to a "Democrats-only" strategy, painting himself into a left corner where presidential success or failure would depend on how well he did on Capitol Hill—Buddha was in chains there, too. After hugging Foley and the rest on camera the morning after, he turned to the mass of press surrounding him.

The first question that morning was from a reporter asking when Clinton would redeem his campaign promise to issue an Executive Order ending discrimination against homosexual men and lesbians in the U. S. military. Clinton said he had no timetable in mind, but he intended to "firmly proceed . . . after consulting with military leaders."

It was as if he had made a bargain with the devil. "I can make you president," ol' Lucifer said, "and I will ask you for only one thing." That would be a deal Clinton could not refuse. The devil materialized again on Inauguration Day, using only four words: "Gays in the military!"

The new president thought he could walk on one of the most painful, most symbolic fault lines in America, a nerve exposed first in the 1960s when homosexuals began demonstrating to end discrimination based on what they called "sexual orientation." In Washington that day in 1992, the deputy minority leader of the House, a Georgia Republican named Newt Gingrich, watching the president-elect on television with Foley and Mitchell, thought about the same thing as Al From: "He's going to govern from the left"—and began offering nickel bets that Clinton would be a one-term president. By the summer of 1994, Gingrich was offering four-to-one odds that Clinton was finished—and thinking that just maybe he himself was going to be the Speaker of a Republican-controlled House of Representatives. Maybe even president, one day.

3.
Bill Clinton,
Bothered and Bewildered

So, Mr. Clinton went to Washington.

Vice President Albert Gore Jr., who was brought up in Washington, the son of a senator, and came back as a member of Congress himself in 1977, hesitated a bit when I asked him the difference between the capital city he came to and the one Bill Clinton came to fifteen years later. "The whole country is different," said Gore. "All these body blows to the sense of national well-being. The economic transformations. The disorienting effect of all this electronic information."

I tried again, asking whether any president could control the kind of people who made it to the House and Senate these days: "The Congress now, is it two parties or 535 individuals?"

"Both," he said.

I must have looked blank. "Do you know Prigogine's work?" he asked.

My expression did not change, so Gore went on, telling me that Ilya Prigogine is a Belgian scientist (Russian-born) who won a Nobel Prize in 1977 for his work in thermodynamics. "He proved that if you look at a system with more and more energy and matter coming in, it will spontaneously reorganize itself into a more complicated system," said Gore. "Something different will come out, but what it is can't be predicted beforehand."

He drew a diagram, a pipeline leading into and out of an empty chamber. Washington is the chamber. More molecules were coming in— more matter, more energy, more heat, more information, new news cycles, new action-reaction-reaction-action. Just more stuff, faster and faster. Pow! Something happens inside—Gore scrawls a new world in the chamber— and then something differ-

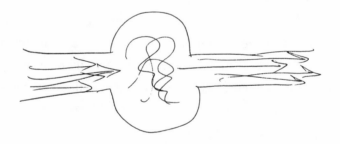

ent comes out the other end, which in this case is what America senses beyond the Beltway. Inside there are new men, new women, new media, new money, new information, new relationships, new sounds, new smells, new laws—and, after the 1994 elections, a new nastiness. A new Washington. Outside the chamber, which these days is called "Beyond the Beltway," Route 495, the peripheral road around Washington—it makes no sense to beholders—first there is confusion, then contempt.

(Not able to vouch for the validity of Gore's interpretation of Prigogine's work, I tracked down the scientist and associates working at the University of Texas. "Yes, good. Quite accomplished," was their surprised reaction to the vice president's analysis.)

Pow! A money-information complex instead of the old military-industrial complex. Public opinion democracy—government of the polls, by the polls, and for the polls. Numbers make news. Money makes numbers. Three trillion dollars. Forty-eight percent. Polls are the new constituencies. Fame is money. Reporters get more of both than the people they cover. Everyone is the same size on television. One man plus a fax becomes a majority. Now an electronic beltway separates the city in the chamber from the nation. The Republicans, losers all these years, announce the public is always right, an updated version of the king can do no wrong. And the always-right public turns right, to Newt Gingrich using venomous words like "sick" and "grotesque" and "immoral" to describe anyone who disagreed with him, promising, above all, to punish the old Congress and the old ways—maybe even roll back the 1960s and make a new time like the old days when women and blacks and gays and the young, too, knew their place.

Listening inside the Beltway, before and after the midterm elections, you would have thought that Bill and

Hillary Rodham Clinton came to town in beads and bell-bottoms. During a closed committee meeting considering the universal health care plan produced by Hillary Clinton, a Democratic senator of tenure and stature blurted out a Rip Van Winkle theory: "Jesus Christ! What we're dealing with here are two VISTA volunteers who went to Arkansas twenty years ago and came back here thinking it's still the sixties."

Life in those years speeded up and heated up in Prigogine Washington. The capital is information-driven now—or driven crazy by instant information. Decision-making is high-speed and interactive; analysis and adjustment are reactive and continuous. "News cycles," which not so long ago meant information produced to meet the needs of afternoon and morning newspapers and the evening network news, has exploded into something like a million car radios stuck on "scan."

"These changes," said Gore, "are not friendly to the linear debate envisioned by the Founding Fathers."

How did it look to the forty-second president?

"I was bewildered," said Clinton when I asked. In fact, he was still using the same word in conversations at the end of each of his first two years in the White House. His wife, Hillary Rodham Clinton, has also used the same word during conversations with me and others that seemed to inevitably turn to the subject of softening her public image. I was interested in the word and its definition because both the Clintons generally use language so well. According to Merriam-Webster's *Collegiate Dictionary*, "bewilder" means "1: to cause to lose one's bearings 2: to perplex or confuse esp. by a complexity, variety, or multitude of objects or considerations."

"I must say there's a lot I have to learn about this town," President Clinton said after his first hundred days in office. Before coming he had promised a hundred days to match Franklin Roosevelt's legislative rush of 1933, days that changed the United States. Instead, he played the new kid, a true freshman president. "Home Alone 3," wrote Tom Shales, the television critic of the *Washington Post,* of Clinton's first Oval Office speech to the nation on February 15, 1993. Sitting behind President Kennedy's desk with a bust of Abraham Lincoln behind him, Clinton looked too small for the setting. He could not shake the troubles of the gays-in-the-military debate, which he had started. The administration was moving clumsily on appointments, leaving Republican holdovers in key slots across the government—"because Clinton couldn't get around to naming any Democrats" wrote Mary McGrory of the *Washington Post*—and some of them were spending their time investigating or harassing the president, particularly on the Whitewater affair and the relationships between the Clintons and failed savings-and-loan operations back in Arkansas.

He was making a fool of himself, actually: After dropping his nomination of a black woman, Lani Guinier, as an assistant attorney general, he said he still thought she was a fine choice, the kind of person he would lend five thousand dollars if she asked. Among the things that bewildered him was the resonance of the presidential voice. Like most of us, he had talked and talked, with nobody much listening. But when the president speaks, people hear—and they act. So thousands of Haitians began building boats to flee to the United States after he denounced the Bush administration for turning back refugees from that wretched island. He was shocked when the Dow Jones Industrial Average dropped eighty-three points the morning after he talked of new taxes on the people George Bush liked to call "the investing classes"—most of the rest of us just call them rich. Then there were the miles of paper and days of television time devoted to whether or not Clinton held up air traffic at the Los Angeles airport by getting a $200 haircut from a Beverly Hills stylist called to do his thing on *Air Force One* one May day in 1993.

Later that month, *Time* magazine ran a tiny photograph of Clinton on its cover under the headline, "The Incredible Shrinking President." A week later, the president appointed a new special counsel, David Gergen, a sometime journalist and commentator who had handled image-making for three Republican presidents, Bush, Ronald Reagan, and Richard Nixon. In offering the job, Clinton had said: "I need you to interpret Washington for me."

In conversation with the president, I turned the subject to whether or not he was really prepared for the job. He was the most gifted politician (or candidate) of his generation: self-created, seeming almost Rooseveltian in his political skills, a man with the smarts and the guts to understand that the final true qualification for the presidency was winning it—and figuring out a way to do that, not an easy task for the governor of a small state like Arkansas. But my questions and others he did not like signaled doubts about his capability to govern. Not that anyone could be fully prepared for the most powerful job in the world; the presidency is sui generis. I agree with something Clinton's hero, President Kennedy, told a historian in 1962: "No one has a right to grade a president—not even poor James Buchanan—who has not sat in this office, examined the mail and information that came across his desk, and learned how he made his decisions."

But we still try. I asked the most scholarly man in the Senate, Daniel Patrick Moynihan of New York, who had served Kennedy, whether he thought Clinton was prepared. "No," he said. Then, he added: "Worse. He thought he was prepared."

Clinton himself answered the same question this way: "I think on the substance and the issues, I was prepared to be president." What surprised him most, he went on, was the attitude of the Washington press corps. He assumed that what he considered harsh campaign coverage—"combative and intensely negative," were his words—would end when he went to the White House. "I was wrong . . . I wasn't prepared for it. I was bewildered by it . . . I fought it by working harder."

"Hard work" is the last refuge of the incompetent. The press, a roaring pain in the ass in the best of times, is the easiest target for the bewildered. President Clinton is not incompetent, but he is insecure and defensive. He spends altogether too much time feeling sorry for himself—a common condition for presidents.

Clinton never seems to stop talking about how hard he works and how many things he is trying to do. He did it three times in one forty-minute interview with me.

"I'm not perfect, but I work hard and I get things done," was the way he put it the first time. Each time he followed it with some variation of: "If a Republican had reduced the deficit, shrunk the size of the federal government, sparked a new wave of recovery, passed a crime bill with lots of tough punishment and capital punishment and stuff, they'd be running that Republican for God. You know?" At his worst, about half the time, Clinton talks as if he were being paid by the hour—rather than for his judgment and the democratic faith that he can find the way to bring out the best in the American people.

He can't keep up. I'm not sure anyone can. The checks and balances and cumbersome processes devised in the eighteenth century to slow down governance are mowed down now like slalom flags snapping under an out-of-control skier. It may often seem to "normal Americans," to use Gingrich's term, that nothing is happening in Washington, but to the players there too much is happening too quickly to be seen, much less understood.

One small example: The old newspaper staple, the story-behind-the-story, has been overtaken and passed by the story-before-the-story. When a couple of *Los Angeles Times* reporters, William Rempel and Douglas Frantz, were in Little Rock in the fall of 1993, checking out a new round of rumors about Governor Clinton's sex life, a Republican congressman from California, Robert Dornan, went on Rush Limbaugh's radio program and announced that the paper was about to publish a story on the new allegations.

Another example: Clinton's first shot in anger was to order a Tomahawk missile strike from U. S. warships in the Persian Gulf on the headquarters of Iraq's intelligence agency in Baghdad—in retaliation, the president said, for a planned assassination of former president George Bush during a visit to Kuwait. Anxious to announce the strike live on the nightly news, Clinton was frustrated because he could not get information on whether or not the missiles hit their target. His counselor, David Gergen, finally suggested calling CNN rather than the CIA. At 6:30 P.M., Tom Johnson, the president of Cable News Network, was able to tell the president of the United States that the Tomahawks had indeed hit their target. Then the commander in chief went live on CNN (and the three networks) to announce the news to the people who had told him.

One of the president's men, George Stephanopoulos, offered his own take on the speed-up. He said that although only six hundred thousand people watch CNN, they are the right six hundred thousand—or the wrong ones, depending on your viewpoint. "News people and the networks watch all day, so they think whatever happened on CNN is old news," he said—which drives the networks to create something new and different each night, even if viewers, home after a day of their own work, have no idea what CNN did that day.

The president, any president, has lost one of the office's critical powers: control over the flow of information to the people of the United States. What the people know and when they know it is the engine of democracy.

Once upon a time, the president had his hand on the throttle. No more. That was dramatized for me on a Monday morning in October of 1993, when I appeared on NBC's *Today* show. My segment came after three wives of American soldiers in Somalia were on, one of them crying, saying that their husbands were going to be killed and their children would be orphans. All that, they said, was because President Clinton had sent their men to Africa on what was supposed to a humanitarian United Nations mission to a country being decimated by famine and war. Then, thanks to another miracle of modern technology, the husbands called in from Mogadishu on cellular phones to say that their commander in chief had told them there was no danger but that people were shooting at them. My first thought was that Lincoln and Roosevelt were lucky there were no cellulars at Gettysburg or on the beaches at Normandy.

Who needs that? Television personalizes news and its effects on both watchers and watched. Eighteen U. S. Army Rangers were later killed on a single day in Mogadishu, an event that shook Clinton badly. He put off meeting with the families of the dead men. Months later, he extended his hand to Herbert Shughart, father of one of the men. Shughart refused to take it. "You are not fit to be president of the United States," said the grieving father. "The blame for my son's death rests . . . with you."

Since the advent of direct satellite transmission from any place on the planet, there really has been no such thing as geography on television. Inevitably, geographical representation no longer matters as much as it did to the Founding Fathers and the generations of politicians who followed them. Many of a new breed of self-selected politicians do not come from anyplace really. Yale, maybe, or Harvard or celebrity, but not from a town or city in ever-changing districts—those are just places to leave and pump in new information from the center. In Washington, many of the members of new Congresses spend their days and nights searching for an issue, the kind that can get them on television.

The jargon is "owning an issue"—anything from Afghanistan to Zaire, from flat taxes to gun control will do—and the rules of the game call for respecting the issue turf of colleagues who have already staked their claims. The picture of how it works is on television most nights, on *The McNeill/Lehrer News Hour* or *Nightline.* Television is interested in familiar expertise and balanced opinion, but that balance has nothing to do with geography and often has little to do with partisan politics.

There is a new political language in the capital: Words, names, ideas, and places have been replaced by numbers. Poll numbers and dollars. That part of it Clinton got right away: He often treats polls as his real constituency. Back at his desk in the White House after going to France for elaborately staged ceremonies commemorating the fiftieth anniversary of D-day landings in Normandy on June 6, 1994, Clinton looked at the numbers, banged his desk, and said: "All that work and my approval went up just 1. 5 percent. Can you believe it?"

The new Washington is information-driven and the most immediately opportune or threatening information is often polls. This is the capital city as described by Peter Hart, who collects numbers for the Democratic Party and for the president:

"The world of public opinion has come into great collision with the art of governance. In the old Washington there were two or three polls, principally Gallup and Harris, and each one took a couple of weeks to do, going door-to-door. And what private polling there was went to the president or the president's party. . . . Now, with new kinds of telephones and computers for tabulation, in a half-hour you can come back and say, 'This is what the public thinks.' And the polling is 'spin numbers'; that is, 'advocacy analysis' done by the parties, by associations, by corporations, who can use or release only the questions or answers that suit their narrow purposes, which often comes down to changing a number or a word in complex legislation that means someone or some interest gets a few million dollars or someone else does not. At the same time, the networks and the press are polling, because it is prestigious to have your own poll, like every hospital that wants Medi-vac helicopters."

Exactly. On the press side, numbers tend to sweep away editors, reporters and sometimes common sense and what used to be called judgment. The seductive hint of science and certainty relieves decision-makers of responsibility; they can lay blame on the numbers. The statistical alchemy can be used to minimize human error— and humans, too.

One year before the 1996 elections, in November of 1995, *Time* magazine and CNN announced something they called "Election Monitor," continuous polling of a fixed sample of five thousand voters. "It'll give us a moving picture of voter opinion," said Stephen Koepp, *Time*'s overseer of polling. His counterpart at CNN, Tom Hannon, added: "We're going to use these surveys as the foundation of a lot of our reporting . . . "

"It is," Hart said, in deliberate understatement, "difficult to put a long-range plan into effect in a world of short-term impressions."

The way the survey impression game has evolved inside the electronic beltway was dramatized in late October of 1995 when President Clinton and the Republican leaders of Congress were jockeying for leverage over the Republicans' wild-swinging initiatives to balance the federal budget and cut both taxes and future Medicare expenditures. On October 26, Speaker Gingrich surprised a lot of people with a semi-hysterical news conference denouncing a *New York Times*/CBS News poll published and broadcast that day reporting or indicating that two-thirds of the American people are more concerned about cuts in Medicare than in balancing the federal budget. Only one-quarter of us, according to the *Times* and CBS, were more concerned that day about balancing the national checkbook.

"This poll is a disgraceful example of disinformation," said Gingrich. "What we get are deliberately rigged questions that are totally phony . . . " The question (one of the ninety-six in the questionnaire) that upset Gingrich was this one: "If you had to choose, would you prefer balancing the federal budget or preventing Medicare from being significantly cut?"

Whoa! The questions and the numbers may be lousy or silly or ephemeral, but they are not "phony." They exist. Since there was no way that a poll released on the morning of the vote was likely to change the minds of

significant numbers of congressman, there had to be another reason the speaker was so agitated. And that reason was that balanced budget fever itself had been poll-
driven from the beginning. The "Contract with America"
had been a product of polling. And since that time Gingrich and other Republicans had repeatedly expressed
wonder that anyone in their right mind could oppose a
balanced budget, which they said again and again "is
supported by 80 percent of the American people."

I don't know where the number eighty came from, but
it existed because Gingrich said it did. (I also do not
know any of the X-percent of the American people who
believe Elvis is alive.) But it doesn't matter where poll
numbers come from. Say them and they exist—unless
they are superseded by new numbers. Gingrich, having
taken the balanced budget argument beyond economics
and beyond ideology (and common sense) to that highest of the politicians' icons, Public Opinion, had been
shaken by this one-day challenge to his magic number
by the dread liberal media.

Everybody has a number in the democracy of public
opinion. The electronic din is a great equalizer. The
president and Rush Limbaugh, the *New York Times,* the
National Enquirer and the CIA, the Pharmaceutical
Manufacturers Association, Larry King, soldiers' wives,
and you and I find out at the same time these days: All
information is created equal. So, it seems, are all "surveys" and all "faxes," all crimes and all faces on televi-

sion, whether it is the president declaring war or the sol-
dier's wife who follows him saying her children need
daddy at home. This particular president senses that
sometimes he is least among equals, saying: "I have a far
higher level of accountability for the information I put
out than almost anyone else in the country. . . . The standards for public conduct are higher today than they have
been in the past. But the perception is that it's worse because we set these standards and then the minute someone varies from them, you know—so that's frustrating."

I agree with that, although I know I am part of the
problem. The press is a principal enforcer of those new
standards. Righteously and regularly, we go as far as technology allows, with little thought of consequences beyond our own career advancement. Our excesses of mor-
alism in Washington are ironic, too, because, as far as I
can tell, the public ethic actually is higher than the private ethic in this country—but there are more laws, reg-
ulations, and reporters surrounding the men and
women in public life.

The place looks quite strange to others. Simon Hog-
gart, a talented former British correspondent in Washington who now covers Parliament for one of Britain's
national papers, the *Guardian,* wrote this in the *New York
Times:* "What do you guys think you're doing? . . . You
demand total financial integrity from your politicians,
while agreeing to a system that requires them to raise
millions of dollars to have any hope of being elected. You

say in effect, 'We will vote for you if you woo us at tremendous expense, but every penny you raise must be unblemished. . . . ' Washington appears to run by a set of mores and customs as obscure to the world as the social practices of Trobriand Islanders. For example, we are told, Bernard Nussbaum had to resign as White House counsel because he took part in 'inappropriate briefings.' I can't imagine a single head of government—certainly not here in Britain or even in largely scandal-free nations like Canada and Finland—who could survive if that particular charge were thought damaging."

The poll explosion has evolved, too, in a way that allows reporters to judge the performance and words of public officials by changing numbers and public mood. Clinton, of course, stiffens at the thought that he cares about or uses such things for his own political purposes. Though his personal pollster, Stanley Greenberg, has gotten almost two million dollars a year from the Democratic National Committee and though I did not ask about it, the president made a point of saying this to me: "I can tell you categorically that I do not use polls to decide what position to take. I have used polling information to try to make sure I understand exactly where the American people are, what they know, what they don't know. . . . It's important to know how you're being perceived and what people think—where they're getting their information. But that can't affect the search for what's right for America."

Perhaps. But there is a good deal of evidence and tes-
timony that in this White House, polls (and focus groups)
are the search for America—with the President as the
facilitator-in-chief of public opinion. Bill Clinton is a surfer
politician, waiting on his board, looking back toward the
horizon, confident he will see the first hint of the next
big wave, then ride high wherever it takes him. The wave
broke to the right in the 1994 elections, so he brought in
a conservative pollster named Dick Morris, a Republican whose most important client was Trent Lott of Mississippi, the deputy majority leader of the Senate. Morris had served Clinton once before, when he came back
after being defeated for a second term as governor in
1980. The new political best friend promoted a strategy
called "triangulation," a fancy word for getting halfway
between Republican positions and Democratic positions
and pretending to be above partisan politics—running
in place against both the Republicans and Democrats in
Congress. The president did not move or talk as much as
usual, betting that voters and the press would turn their
energy—most of it negative—to the odd couple conservative leadership of the new Congress. "Clinton's just
part of the crowd now," in the words of Judy Woodruff of
CNN in late September of 1995. That worked for a time,
and soon enough, by the end of 1995, Newt Gingrich and
Bob Dole had lower approval ratings than Bill Clinton. In
fact, Gingrich, the principal architect of the Republicans'
1994 victory, was turning out to be at least as disliked

and distrusted as Clinton was—the Speaker was a wave that just might carry the president back into office in 1996.

Inside the White House, watching for big waves and the effects of new public information and opinion systems, one of Clinton's men, Deputy National Security Adviser Samuel (Sandy) Berger, said something worth remembering: "Machines can't think, but they change the way people do." Added Hart: "Clinton is a president who doesn't need new information or more information. He explores it all . . . (and) the effects are dramatic, short-term impulses, which means a constantly changing course."

Reading the Sunday papers as the president prepared a budget offered a glimpse of how polling shapes any politician's world as surely as war and elections. Among the public opinion "findings" reported that day in just two newspapers, the *New York Times* and the *Los Angeles Times,* were these: Forty-one percent of Americans believe that foreign aid is the largest item in the federal budget, according to the Program on International Policy Attitudes of the University of Maryland; Americans believe that 40 percent of United Nations peacekeeping forces are U. S. troops, according to the Center for International and Security Studies; one of four Americans believe "the United Nations poses a threat to the Constitutional rights enjoyed by average Americans"; better than two out of five believe the same thing of the United States government itself, according to a Times-Mirror

Survey; and, said Times-Mirror, 12 percent more Americans believed that President Clinton was doing a good job than believed it thirty days before.

Great stuff! All numbers are created equal. In fact, foreign aid accounts for less than 1 percent of the budget, and fewer than 4 percent of UN peacekeepers are Americans. But whether they're accurate or silly or unfathomable, survey numbers become facts of a kind. They are the bases of a new kind of democracy. Public opinion democracy. It does not matter whether the numbers are right or wrong, or even within the bounds of sanity. They can still be used, as if scientific, to justify any position, any action, any "leader." Survey numbers, generated from God knows where, have become the first and last court of political appeal in the democracy. A politician has to decide whether to tell constituents or voters that they have no idea what they are talking about on, say, foreign aid—or he can say that foreign aid is a mess, waste, and all that, and he intends to clean up that mess in their name.

Bill Clinton, who already has new polls of his own, is a man who likes old cars—he owns a '65 Mustang—and that's part of the reason he wanted to stop that day in Pennsylvania. Many men do, because you can open the hood and understand how the thing works. The same is true of old typewriters. But open the hood of a new car or a computer, or open up the Prigogine chamber called Washington—and it's bewildering!

4.
Passion for Distinction

In Arkansas, Bill Clinton was a new type: a smart boy, born poor but rich in credentials earned, a self-selected candidate born in a town called Hope, but really from Georgetown, Yale, and Oxford. "You have to admire him," said Robert Shapiro, the chief economist of the Progressive Policy Institute, which is affiliated with the Democratic Leadership Council. "He got elected five times by telling people he was the smartest guy in the state."

But there were a lot like him in Washington: Even though he was a new boy, he was back among his own kind. Most of the capital's elect are smart (at least in the IQ sense of the word), self-selected career candidates who have traded almost everything in their lives to indulge what one of Clinton's predecessors, John Adams, called "a passion for distinction."

Clinton is just the most successful of this baby-boom meritocracy, the first to go all the way by understanding that the best way to win is to run again and again. In

Washington, he was a stranger among his own kind, gregarious loners who began running for president as teenagers. Clinton's high school principal had to limit the number of organizations a student could join to stop him from running for president of every one. Many are serving constituencies of polls. Ultimately and inevitably, some serve only themselves in the quest for an issue that can lift them above the crowd, something that can get them on television. "They're political entrepreneurs," said George Stephanopoulos, who had served on Dick Gephardt's staff before joining the Clinton campaign. "After twelve years of Republicans in the White House, Democratic members of Congress had gotten used to being on their own."

The new president did not seem to get that during the two years he lived with the Democratic 103rd Congress. He looked for Democrats and Republicans, northerners and southerners in the Capitol. But what he actually found inside the buildings on Capitol Hill were one hundred quasi-presidents in the Senate and 435 mini-presidents in the House of Representatives—all of them served by staffs as big as real presidents had only thirty years ago. The discipline of the new 104th Congress restrained some of the more entrepreneurial Republicans, but the overall goal of the membership still seemed to be to get on television.

Most of the Democrats of the 103rd and many of the new Republicans of the 104th had no strong political base other than the public opinion of the moment—not if a political "base" is geographic or is defined as the people who are for you right or wrong. Ronald Reagan had a base, Americans who were with him no matter what he said or did. Senator Jesse Helms of North Carolina, on the right, has a base. On the left, Senator Paul Wellstone, a Minnesota true believer in good old liberalism, has a base. They don't need polls. But Bill Clinton, who says he feels all pain, probably has less of a core constituency—below 20 percent in some of his own polls—than the 25 percent or so Richard Nixon still had the day he resigned the presidency. The Democratic president seemed to have nothing but the vestiges of the coalition that carried Franklin Roosevelt to power. By 1994, all that Democrats had for sure were an uneasy minority coalition of blacks, public employees (particularly unionized bureaucrats and civil servants), Jews, and aging ideological cadres who used to be branded as the high-fashion wearers of radical chic.

So young Republicans got to Washington in 1995 by attacking tired Democratic old-timers who had lost touch with new times and old constituencies, and the credentialed career class that was more concerned with polls and television sound-bites than with the boredom of spending time with car dealers and insurance agents back home somewhere. That aspect of the Republican rise is hardly new. In 1835, in *Democracy in America,* Alexis de Tocqueville wrote that in America, "It was by promising to weaken the government that one won the right to control it." Two years later, John L. O'Sullivan, the editor of *U. S. Magazine and Democratic Review* wrote: "The best government is that which governs least."* In 1849, Henry David Thoreau, in his tract "Civil Disobedience," shortened that to: "That government is best which governs not at all"—long before Jimmy Carter, Ronald Reagan, Bill Clinton, and Newt Gingrich adapted that instinct to their own purposes.

One hundred and sixty years later, the route to power may be the same, but the people traveling it are different. Neither Reagan nor Clinton nor Gingrich came from the landed and established class. Their rise represented a democratization of political power that some think has, with the power of new technologies, grown into something shattering.

"Is this democratization or disintegration?" said Clinton's White House counsel, Lloyd Cutler, a fifty-year veteran of capital ways and wars, when I asked him about wider distribution of power in today's Washington. The disturbance of congressional order had been going on at least since 1977, when the president of that year's Democratic freshman class explained the simple political reason that he and his classmates did not feel bound to President Carter: "Remember, most of us ran ahead of

---

* O'Sullivan, quite a phrase-maker, also coined the term, "Manifest Destiny."

Carter in our districts, so we feel pretty independent of the old straight-loyalty-to-leadership appeal." That class president was a new California congressman named Leon Panetta, who became chief of staff in the Clinton White House in 1994.

The Democratic leaders of Congress, with whom Clinton made common cause for the first two years, did not know how to lead because they had never done it. "The word partisanship is overused here," said Secretary of the Interior Bruce Babbitt before the midterm elections. "The most striking thing when we came here was that there was no leadership in the Congress. The institution had been disaggregated. There was a different coalition for every issue—like a pick-up basketball game. You were always starting over, putting 535 cards on the wall every day."

Still, for most of Clinton's first year in the White House, the Foley-Gephardt-Mitchell "Democrats only" congressional strategy worked reasonably well. The comprehensive health care plan constructed by Mrs. Clinton was an obvious failure, though it seemed for a time that the administration had moved that national debate from "Whether or not" to "When and how." But aside from that, the president and congressional Democrats were able to write new law that produced deficit reduction, trade liberalization, earned income-tax credits for the so-called "working poor," some control over sales of assault weapons and other street guns—and a glowing headline in *Congressional Quarterly:* CLINTON RECOVERS FROM EARLY STUMBLES, ENDING YEAR IN COMMAND OF CONGRESS.

His approval rate then was up to 53 percent—not dazzling perhaps, but a lot better than the Congress and the press in the same polls. Economic statistics were moving, too. In December of 1993, the Consumer Confidence Index of the U. S. Conference Board jumped eleven points, with the number of households reporting that things were looking "good" rising from 60 percent to 71 percent. Clinton seemed to have broken "gridlock," the Washington stasis that had doomed the presidency of George Bush. More than 86 percent of the bills President Clinton had sent to Congress had passed in both houses. That was better than John Kennedy had ever done and within a percentage point or two of Lyndon Johnson's best year.

They were talking second term in Washington. A lot of Republicans, Newt Gingrich loudest among them, were saying that if Clinton was not stopped, the country might be looking at eight years of Clinton and eight more of a Gore presidency. Some had added another eight years for Hillary Rodham Clinton. They were kidding. Maybe.

That was the peak, about as far as Clinton could go with the Democratic Congress. He mouthed the words of least government when he had to, but by instinct he was a government activist, wanting government to do good things. But such good things cost money, and his kind of activism was dead—probably for a generation. It was killed with brilliance and malice aforethought by the huge deficit spending begun by President Ronald Reagan—three trillion dollars in twelve years—and resulting budget cuts and caps. In domestic affairs, at least, being president had become a zero-sum game.

As for foreign policy, where modern presidents have generally been able to avoid advice and counsel from Congress, many Washingtonians thought this president's foreign policy was pretty well defined by a *Los Angeles Times* headline on September 23, 1993: CLINTON TELLS U. N. U. S. WILL LEAD BUT WILL LIMIT ITS ROLE. Ah, limited leadership.

But, in fact, there were a couple of American triumphs in the world. Clinton muscled through Senate approval of the North American Free Trade Agreement, a leftover Republican initiative creating a United States-Canada-Mexico economic alliance, and he presided over a dramatic hand-shaking-for-television peace agreement signed at the White House by Prime Minister Yitzhak Rabin of Israel and Yassir Arafat, the leader of the Palestine Liberation Organization.

Versions of that triumph were repeated later in Haiti, Northern Ireland, and even in the Balkan civil war called Bosnia. Clinton learned to play an important role in foreign policy as theater, but only after showing himself to be weak and uncertain when the subject shifted offshore, repeatedly wrong footing himself in cycles of threat-deadline-backdown—particularly when it came to war in Bosnia and trade with China. His own staff and advisers admitted that his eyes seemed to literally glaze over at the mention of Bosnia or Somalia, or darted around the room when the subject turned to China or Korea. In frustration, one of the president's men blurted out to him: "You're going to put yourself in the position of nuking North Korea, do you understand that? One threat leads to another. You have to think ahead."

In the second session of the 103rd Congress, the Republicans made their move. In August of 1994, House Republicans, led by Gingrich, ambushed Clinton, collecting enough wandering Democratic votes to defeat the president's omnibus crime bill—a bill that included an amendment, approved earlier, to ban the sale of nineteen types of assault weapons. Speaker Foley and Gephardt came to the White House to tell Clinton what he should have known all along, that they did not control enough votes to save the bill and him—but they could get fifty more votes if he agreed to drop the assault weapons ban. He might have done it except for the fact that the ban's principal sponsor, a congressman from Brooklyn named Charles Schumer, once shared a Capitol Hill apartment with three other members, one of them Leon Panetta. Schumer's old roommate got him in to see the president. Clinton listened to the leaders, then he listened to Schumer, finally standing up and saying: "Okay, we'll do it. I'll fight."

Ten days later he won. It was about the last famous victory of his first two years—and the end of the confining alliance he had made two years before in Little Rock. On the first Sunday of that October, Speaker Foley, in a tough re-election fight back home in the state of Washington, was on NBC's *Meet the Press.* He was asked, "Is your close relationship with President Clinton a detriment?" He answered: "I don't know."

Then he added: "My district comes first."

Ah, the old "Bill who?" The president was on his own. He did not know where to turn—until the votes were counted.

5.
Smart and Smarter and Too Smart

In fact, Clinton inherited little of the presidential power that once came with being leader of his party. It may have been impossible for any Democratic president to take control of a party that was ideologically broad enough to stretch from Maxine Waters of California on the left to Richard Shelby of Alabama on the right. (Shelby became a Republican after the 1994 elections.) Somewhere in the middle was Jim Cooper, a six-term, forty-one-year-old Democratic congressman from Tennessee. "A good friend," said Clinton.

But his friend Cooper was among the first to openly oppose the Clinton health care plans and voted against the Clinton crime bill, too. Part of the price Clinton paid for positioning himself with the congressional leaders was that his intraparty disagreements were with his natural and old allies from the Democratic Leadership Council, of which he was once chairman, including Representatives Cooper and Dave McCurdy of Oklahoma, and Senators Sam Nunn of Georgia, John Breaux of Louisiana, and David Boren of Oklahoma. One conservative Democrat, Representative W.J. "Billy" Tauzin of Louisiana, offered this advice to other candidates in 1994: "Get away from Bill Clinton. Stop voting for Clinton policies."*

This was the text of Clinton's friend Jim Cooper's principal television commercial as he ran for Vice President Gore's old Senate seat that year:

> Of course we're all angry at Washington. So is Jim Cooper, but he's done more than talk. . . . Across town, the Washington power structure was so frightened by the Cooper (health) plan they never allowed a vote on it. . . . But he stood like a rock. And a president retreated.

The White House's reaction to all that was to send Vice President Gore home to Tennessee to campaign and raise money (more than $250,000) for Cooper. "What kind of politics is that?" I asked Clinton. His answer on Cooper was no different than his answer on Aristide: "If it works and gets him elected, that's his business."

It did not work. Congressman Cooper, a product of Shelbyville (population: 14,049), Groton, Harvard, and Oxford, won only 39 percent of the vote against a Republican lawyer/actor, Fred Thompson—he was in *The Search for Red October*—who wore red flannel shirts and

---

* In August of 1995, Representative Tauzin, who won re-election, switched parties, becoming a Republican.

campaigned in a leased Chevy pickup truck, more or less denying that he even knew the way to Washington. In the real world, he had earned $207,803 in Washington as a lobbyist during the eighteen months before the election. Tocqueville would have perfectly understood Thompson's campaign against the government he wanted to join. After his election, the Republican in the red-flannel shirt returned to his precampaign transportation, a chauffeured Lincoln Town Car.

Thompson was an exception. Most of the newcomers in 1995 were true believers who really did want to break up the government, at least they did before they became part of it. The House of Representatives went from 257 Democrats and 176 Republicans in the 103rd Congress to 233 Republicans and 201 Democrats (and one Independent) in the 104th Congress. Newt Gingrich replaced Tom Foley, who lost his district back in the state of Washington, becoming the first Republican Speaker of the House since 1950. The Senate went from 56 Democrats and 44 Republicans to 54 Republicans and 46 Democrats. Republican Bob Dole of Kansas replaced George Mitchell of Maine as majority leader.

6.
Lifestyles of Rich and Famous Correspondents

The dominant members of the press corps in the new Washington have credentials as good as Jim Cooper's— or Bill Clinton's. And more than a few make a great deal more money than either Fred Thompson or, for that matter, the president of the United States. For the "reporters" who are television regulars, lectures alone can produce more income than the new senator made lobbying, lawyering, and acting. And the celebrities among them are a good deal more famous than the people they cover— when they are in town. "We all know how it works," said David Gergen, who certainly does. The counselor to presidents, magazine editor, and television commentator put it this way: "You write something provocative enough to get on television, then you say something even more provocative on television and then you make the big money on lecture dates around the country."

Flying to a lecture date on USAir, I picked up the magazine in the seat pocket in front of me. *USAir Magazine* is published by a division of the *New York Times,* and in it there was an advertisement promoting a feature called "Coming Home," in which "Some of today's best-known personalities" write or are interviewed about where they come from or where they live now. Twelve of the nineteen celebrities featured in the ad were journalists. The list was headed, alphabetically, by actors Lauren Bacall and Kenneth Branagh, then in the same order came: Art Buchwald, Katie Couric, Michael Kinsley, Jane Pauley, George Plimpton, Anna Quindlen, Cokie Roberts, Tim Russert, Diane Sawyer, Gloria Steinem, Gay Talese, George Will.

Anthony Lake, Clinton's national security adviser, who, like Gergen, began his advising in the Nixon White House, offered this take on how things have changed: "When I first came here, if you wanted to know what a reporter really thought about the people and issues he covered, you had to get drunk with him. Maybe a couple of times. Now I just turn on television to find out what they think."

When Lake was last in town, working for President Jimmy Carter in the 1970s, *New York Times* reporters were generally prohibited from appearing on television. Now the good, gray lady has a public relations agent who sometimes tries to get her reporters on television shows. With good reason. Television exposure makes those reporters more desirable leaking partners for the chatterers on Lake's own staff and the entrepreneurs at the other end of Pennsylvania Avenue.

That night, after talking with Lake, I turned on *The Capital Gang,* a Cable News Network show, and, sure enough, there was Al Hunt, the *Wall Street Journal*'s Washington editor, telling Trent Lott, the Mississippi senator, that he expected him to vote for GATT—the General Agreement on Trades and Tariffs—for the good of the country. And Lott was analyzing the news of the day and asking questions of a gang of four reporters. The world turned upside down.

"Say 'Hi' to your mom," said Hunt to Lott as the show ended. Then a couple of weeks later, Lake himself was on *Meet the Press* being questioned by NBC's Tim Russert, who used to be Pat Moynihan's Tim Russert and Mario Cuomo's Tim Russert, having served on the staffs of both New York's senator and governor before becoming the network's Washington bureau chief. Small world. Cozy, too, as Russert kidded the national security adviser about the ongoing major league baseball strike and Lake responded by wondering whether the Buffalo Bills would ever win football's Super Bowl. None of that could have made any sense to ordinary television watchers if they did not know that Lake is a fanatic fan of the Boston Red Sox and that he spends every minute he can playing something called "Rotisserie Baseball" and Russert is from Buffalo. And that, baffled viewers, is the Washington meaning of the phrase "Inside baseball"— or "Inside the Beltway."

Back at the White House, I asked Tony Lake's assistant, Sandy Berger, a question about the old days and the new: Who was more important now in the making of United States foreign policy, Peter Peterson, the Wall Street wise man and former cabinet officer who is president of the Council on Foreign Relations in New York, or Thomas Friedman, the young *New York Times* reporter who had recently returned from overseas assignments to write of diplomatic and economic affairs in Washington? (Friedman became the *Times'* foreign affairs columnist several months after this conversation.)

Berger just laughed. The question was ridiculous. They have meetings regularly in the White House about what Friedman thinks or what he might do tomorrow. Some of the younger folk at those meetings probably have to be told who Peterson is—or was.

From the president down, they are obsessed with the press in the Clinton White House—as well they should be. This president has not only lost control of the flow of information to the nation, he has little control over the flow of information to himself. Writing of the White House of John F. Kennedy thirty years ago, Hugh Sidey, the designated "insider" of *Time* and *Life* magazines, said: "The White House doors were open. . . . A reporter could tour the offices of the intimates—Salinger, Sorensen, O'Donnell, O'Brien, Dungan, Goodwin, Feldman . . . and get precisely the same viewpoint from each man."

In the Clinton White House, the doors are all closed, often because someone inside is on the phone with a favored and famous reporter, giving his version of something that just happened or was about to happen inside the Oval Office. Imagine this, Mom! Here I am chatting with Bob Woodward . . . or Johhny Apple, or talking to Cokie Roberts about what she said on *Nightline.* In the case of Woodward writing his book, *The Agenda,* on Clinton's economic decision-making, the president told his people it was their duty to talk to the reporter, much as they would stand for the National Anthem. The rich and famous of the press, it seems, will still be telling stories of old Bill and Hillary long after this First Couple has retreated home, wherever that is—laughing with the leakers. There are no term limits for reporters.

On a day I was talking to Lake last August, he was in despair over the lead story on page one of the *New York Times.* TOP U. S. OFFICIALS DIVIDED IN DEBATE ON INVADING HAITI, read the headline over the byline of Elaine Sciolino, who wrote:

> "This division became evident, officials said, at a meeting of Clinton's top national security advisers on Tuesday at the White House. The meeting had been called to draw up recommendations for the President.
>
> "Defense Secretary William J. Perry opposed . . .
>
> "But Deputy Secretary Strobe Talbott . . .
>
> "In a sharp exchange, Mr. Perry countered that Mr. Talbott represented a strange morality. He argued that it would be

immoral for the United States not to do whatever it could to
avoid the loss of lives of American soldiers and the expen-
diture of taxpayers' money . . . "

The piece went on for thirty paragraphs, reporting arguments of and between "principals," as the highest officials call each other. There had been only eight people
in the room on the ground floor of the White House, but
the lady from the *Times* got it exactly right, practically
word-for-word—one or more of the eight principals had
passed the recommendations on to the *Times* (and the
world) before they got to the president.

"How? Why?" Lake said. "Who?" Months later, both
the president and Vice President Gore were still talking
about the Sciolino story, telling me in separate interviews
that they thought they were getting close to figuring out
who leaked to her. In reaction to such leaks, dialogue inside the transparent White House was becoming more
and more distorted as the meetings were getting smaller
and smaller and less and less was put in writing to try to
stop leaks. "You lose expertise, you lose precision," said
Lake. "People are afraid to speak their minds, or they
say things precisely because they want them to be in tomorrow's *Washington Post.*"

Clinton came to Washington determined to dominate
or ignore the capital's gigantic press corps. He had, after
all, faced down the national political press corps early in

1992 when reporters had assumed he would quit the pres- idential race in shame after tabloid revelations of his rela- tionship in Little Rock with a woman named Gennifer Flowers, sometimes a television journalist, sometimes a nightclub singer. The boys and girls on the bus, pleased as puppies with themselves and their importance, flocked to New Hampshire to watch him do a Gary Hart—that is, quit with a usable mea culpa. But he stood up there and told them to shove it. With Hillary by his side, he went on CBS's big show, *60 Minutes,* to explain and blur the sto- ries, much preferring public humiliation to private life.

The new president's truest feelings about the press were apparent on his first day in the White House. Clin- ton closed off the door between the sunny ground-level offices of his press staff and the briefing room and re- porters' cubicles, which are mostly underground. "Smells like a gym down there," he told a friend.

However they smell, newspeople work to get in the first word and the last. For President Clinton, the first words from the most important newspaper in the coun- try, the *New York Times,* amounted to shock therapy. "His transition to governance has been filled with mis- steps . . . crab-like retreats from some of his campaign promises," said the lead editorial Clinton saw when he opened the *Times* on January 20, 1993, his inauguration day. Below that, the next headline warned: "No Waver- ing on Gay Soldiers," over an editorial that concluded:

"If Mr. Clinton backs off now, he will have only invited a backlash against gay servicemen and his own enlightened efforts to promote fairness."

Then in the next week, the *Times* offered a series of honeymoon gifts for the new president, making the paper's editorial page editor, Howell Raines, another smart boy from the South, the cursed name of choice in Clinton's bewildered White House:

January 23: "Bill Clinton and his advisers, who promised a departure from the old go-along Washington, didn't get it. . . . Perhaps by now Mr. Clinton has learned that promising to impose high ethical standards on Washington isn't good enough. He has to deliver."

January 25: "'Let us give this capital back to the people to whom it belongs.' Five days after President Clinton thundered those words in his Inaugural Address is none to soon to say, 'Show us what you've got in mind.'"

January 26: "The Clinton administration's erratic approach toward ending the ban on homosexuals in the military could leave one wondering just who's in charge of the armed forces: the generals or their civilian commander-in chief."

January 27: "It's official, Hillary Rodham Clinton . . . will stand with her man, or maybe ahead of him, in formulating health care policy. . . . [This] is more honest than the charade they went through before her independence became a campaign liability and Mrs. Clinton helped get her husband elected by pretending to be what she was not."

January 28: "Bill Clinton's early moves on the budget have been a three-ring circus of novice mistakes."

Still, the new president thought he could get around the White House regulars. On March 20, 1993, he spoke at an annual dinner of denizens of the lower world, the White House Radio and Television Correspondents Association, and said: "You know why I can stiff you on press conferences? Because Larry King liberated me from you by giving me the American people directly."

Apparently no one told him that the American people don't want him in their homes fulltime or that Larry and Oprah and Arsenio Hall don't cover White House briefings and congressional hearings. One can argue about how well or even how much the capital gang covers governance, but they are the only people who do it every day. "You have to understand that a campaign is a one-ring circus," Al From of the DLC told Clinton, who was still having a great deal of trouble with the press months later. "But being president is a thousand-ring circus, a million-ring circus."

Clinton enjoyed the idea, but was overwhelmed by the reality. The resonance of a president's voice still staggered him. He also had trouble accepting the fact that the presidency is a reactive job. There are surprises most every day in this world— fire, flood, war, and treachery, in addition to surveys, special prosecutors, and Republicans—and most of them came to him courtesy of the press, which now includes instantaneous world-girdling satellite television. Like any man of power, he often blames the messenger, complaining loud and often.

And in fact, part of the electronic din in Washington during his first two years were surveys showing that the nightly news shows said "bad" things about this president about twice as often as they reported "good" things. Yet, in his third year, the quieter Clinton was on the nightly news programs about half as much as he had been before—media focus was on Gingrich and Dole and the murder trial of former football hero O. J. Simpson—and his good-bad survey ratings got better and better. His friend Harry Thomason told him, accurately I think: "They kick you into the gutter, but then they feel bad and think, 'He wasn't really a bad guy, was he? He was trying.' And they reach down and help you up."

The president's new stillness was not popular with at least one group of Americans, the White House press corps. What they wanted from Clinton were regular star-vehicle televised press conferences—getting them out of that smelly basement and on television as momentary equals of the president. Clinton continued to resist, telling his own press office people that all the reporters would do was try to trip him up with scandal questions on women and Whitewater, a sticky Arkansas real estate deal in which the Clintons had invested while he was governor. He was exactly right. One of the few conferences he agreed to do was on the evening of March 24, 1994.

"With the Congress beginning its Easter recess tomorrow, this is a good time to assess the real work we are getting done," he began. In that opening statement he touched on the day's events—the assassination of the leading candidate for president of Mexico, an Air Force transport crash, statistics showing two million new jobs in the United States, fighting in Bosnia, nuclear weapons in North Korea, human rights in China, and the return of American troops from Somalia. He reviewed the progress of health care and welfare reform bills, a crime bill, and campaign reform legislation being debated in Congress. "America's efforts have helped to bring much-needed calm to Sarajevo and led to an important political accord between the Bosnian Muslims and Croats," he said. "We'll continue our efforts to stop North Korea's nuclear program and to seek progress on human rights in China. . . . This Friday, a week ahead of schedule, our troops will return home from Somalia."

"Terry?" he said, asking for the first question.

There were twenty-one questions: one on health care, one on American efforts to block the development of nuclear weapons in North Korea, one on the assassination of Luis Donaldo Colosio—and eighteen on Whitewater and Clinton family finances.

He felt the victim, saying: "Let me tell you what my

wife and I spent the '80s doing. I was the lowest-paid governor of any state in the country. I don't complain about
it. I was proud of that. I didn't do it for the money. I
worked on creating jobs and improving education for the
children of my state. My wife worked in a law firm. . . .
She never took any money for any work she did for the
state. . . . Every year she gave an enormous percentage
of her time to public service work, helping children and
helping education . . . "

Not surprisingly, Clinton preferred interviews with
awed local anchorfolk and the electronic stars dancing
along the yellow brick road running between news and
entertainment. He thought it was all the same, all television—and he may well be right. In the world of information overload, does it matter whether the screen is
marked news or entertainment? At the end of the day, as
the British say, if Bill Clinton of Hope, Arkansas, brings
peace and plenty to the world, that achievement may
share billing with the fact that he went on MTV, the
cable rock-music channel, and told the world about his
preference in underwear.

Near the end of a two-hour "Town Hall" meeting with
young people on MTV, the cable music channel, a seventeen-year-old high school junior named Tisha Thompson asked the president what kind of underwear he preferred, boxers or briefs.

"Usually briefs," he answered. Then he added: "I can't
believe she did that."

The rest of the world could not believe he did it.

He is a modern man, sharing, more candid than truthful, and he was having obvious trouble understanding such old things as the majesty of his office. On television, professionals had their way with him. On May 27, 1993, CBS's *This Morning* set up on the White House lawn—invited, of course—with an audience of a couple of hundred tourists. Rattling off a series of poll numbers, the host, Harry Smith, who is paid more than one million dollars a year for doing such things, turned to Clinton and said:

"I know you don't pay attention to this sort of stuff—polls. You never pay attention probably, right?"

The comedy over, Smith turned to the crowd and said:

"The negatives are now higher than the positives in the polls. . . . There's a feeling in the country, and I think the people here reflect it. I think people in America want you to succeed, but I just want a raise of hands this morning—and don't be intimidated just because you're in the Rose Garden—do you feel like he could be doing a better job? Raise your hands if you think so. Don't be intimidated. Don't be intimidated. There's a lot of folks who feel that way. Do you feel like there's a gap between the promises of the campaign and the performance thus far? If you think so, raise your hands. A lot of folks feel that way. What went wrong?"

For any man on the receiving end of the questions and criticism of a zero-tolerance press, the frustration must be explosive—it becomes a question of where and why they blow. Clinton did it in an interview with Jann Wenner and William Greider of *Rolling Stone* magazine. "I have fought more damn battles here for more different things than any president in the last twenty years," he said, "and I have gotten not one damn bit of credit for it from the knee-jerk liberal press and I'm sick and tired of it. I have fought and fought and fought and fought. I get up here every day, and I work till late at night on everything from national service to the budget to the crime bill and all this stuff. . . . If you convince them I don't have any convictions, that's fine, but it's a damn lie."

He had a point. There is a liberal establishment in the press, but it is made up of ingrates like me, who attack the opposition and our own with equal abandon. And there is a conservative establishment, including Rush Limbaugh, who gets more electronic exposure than all the liberals on the continent, the Reverend Pat Robertson, who has his own cable channel, and various bestselling authors and foundation fellows, Charles Murray and William Bennett among them. Three of the leading lights of the "liberal" press, William Safire, Diane Sawyer and John McLaughlin, served together on the White House staff of Richard Nixon. George Will came from the staff of a Republican senator from Colorado, Gordon Allott. But there is a difference in both style and substance: The liberals are more likely to be essayists, while most of the commenting conservatives are pamphleteers, usually ignoring facts or folks damaging to their champions. The writers of the left generally choose argument over power, regularly selling out their friends, while the conservatives do not seem foolish or free enough to bite the hands that feed them so well.

When I asked Clinton about the "transparency of decision-making" in his White House, he didn't shout at me, but he was still obviously upset about the news of a day eighteen months before, saying:

"Too many people leak and too many people talk. . . . A teeny example of that was in this finally, fully-exposed fraud about the so-called haircut story last year—about me keeping people waiting on the airplane, you know. It was false. It wasn't true. There was no two-hundred-dollar haircut and there was no waiting. . . . The president saying that was less weighty than some mole in the FAA . . . that person had just flat-out lied to the press. . . . But all of a sudden that source had more credibility than me personally saying it wasn't true. . . . There have been a lot of other examples I could give you."

I'm sure. But you do not need Diogenes at your side to realize that some of the candid young president's problems with the press are his own problems with the truth, the whole truth, and nothing but the truth. "Which one do you want?"—the punch line of an old courthouse joke is the way reporters describe dealing with this president and his people. "The White House Isn't Telling Us the Truth" was the three-column headline over an opinion piece by Ruth Marcus of the *Washington Post,* describing her nineteen months of covering this president.

"The Pathetic Lies of Bill Clinton" was the headline of an article by Carl Cannon, White House correspondent of the *Baltimore Sun,* in the October 2, 1995, issue of the *Weekly Standard,* a new journal of the right financed by Rupert Murdoch. Among the whoppers chronicled by Cannon was this one by the president in Des Moines, Iowa: "I am the only president who knew something about agriculture when I got here." Oh, dear! This from a man who never had a dirty-hands job and seems never to have heard of such prominent farmers as George Washington, Thomas Jefferson, Herbert Hoover, and Jimmy Carter. Then there was Clinton's assertion concerning his draft-dodging in the Vietnam War: "If I had to do over it again, I might answer the questions a little better. You know, I'd been in public life a long time and no one had ever questioned my role." In fact, his military record, or the lack of one, had been an issue in almost every campaign he ran.

The idea of lying politicians is not new, but printing it is. The modern press, like modern candidates, is more candid. The same things were said of Franklin D. Roosevelt—but in private. Turner Catledge, the White House correspondent of the *New York Times* in the 1930s, once said that FDR's first instinct was to lie, but that halfway through an answer he would realize he could get away with the truth and he would shift gears. Clinton does the same thing, but there is something wrong with his transmission. It sometimes takes him an hour, a day, or a year to shift subtly or grudgingly into the whole truth.

7.
Clinton the
Murderer!

A lot of people hated President Roosevelt, and his wife, many for the very good reason that he was a great man, greatly changing the assumptions and rules of being American. He changed lives. Many hate President Clinton and his wife, too, for reasons that are much less clear or dramatic. He accomplished more than a few things in his first three years in the White House, but none of them have been life-changing for great numbers of his countrymen and women.

One fine August day, I was walking by the Capitol of the United States, when a big auto-horn sent me leaping toward a sidewalk. Safely out of the way, I looked behind me and saw a mysterious black bus pulling up to the curb, something out of a Batman movie. "Impeach Clinton Tour '94." was painted on the side along with this list of presidential transgressions:

"Womanizing . . . Troopergate . . . Deception . . . Abortion . . . Adultery . . . . Bribery . . . Sodomy . . . Fraud . . . ADFA . . . Abuse of U. S. Constitution . . . Obstruction of

Justice . . . Document-Shredding . . . Drug Abuse . . . Tax Evasion . . . Gennifer Flowers . . . Paula Jones."

Quite a list. It turned out the bus was paid for and run by antiabortion groups.

For $19.95, you can buy a video titled *The Clinton Chronicles—An Investigation into the Alleged Criminal Activities of Bill Clinton and His Circle of Power,* financed in part by foundations controlled by a Pennsylvania newspaper owner, Richard Mellon Scaife, reported to be worth eight hundred million dollars—and apparently willing to spend some of that to get rid of Bill Clinton. The eighty-minute tape is produced quite professionally in California and promoted by Jerry Falwell of the Moral Majority on television around the country. The tape explicitly accuses President Clinton of big-time drug dealing and of multiple murder. "The names and faces of the key players who Clinton used to build his Circle of Power," reads the copy on the box, "as well as those who got in his way and lost their jobs, reputations, virtue, and lives! . . . Drug smuggling . . . Money laundering . . . Vince Foster's 'suicide' . . . Gangland slaying."

That kind of hatred seemed blind and irrational to me—and I am sure to most Americans. (There is also an "Only in America" touch on the video, a line saying, "Warning: Federal Law provides severe civil and criminal penalties for unauthorized reproduction, distribution or exhibition . . . ").

There is obviously widespread mistrust of government and the president in the country, a zealous suspicion that seems to begin in the deep and dark visions of small numbers of militants, individuals, and groups who profess to believe that the United States government is engaged in a massive conspiracy to destroy the Constitution, disarm Christian patriots, and turn the country into a police state or turn it over to secret United Nations forces. On another level, the mistrust drops to gripes of other politicians and of reporters about Clinton's manipulation of the truth and the annoying arrogance of Clinton's young White House staff. Some liberals accuse him of selling out to conservatives. Moderates accuse him—and his wife—of being a closet radical. Some northerners do not trust southerners and the way they talk, and some southerners think Clinton is a phony southerner and a phony Baptist, too. Why, one Texan asked me, do you think he never mentions the name of Lyndon Baines Johnson, even when he spoke at the LBJ Library at the University of Texas? Phonies, him and his Yalie wife, too, you hear, with their movie-star friends and their vacations on that haven of ivied elites, Martha's Vineyard. The passion of it all seems out of proportion with the man himself.

Wesley Pruden, the editor of the capital's conservative and distantly second newspaper, the *Washington Times,* wrote a column parroting some of the claims of Clinton-haters and analyzing, quite seriously, "the expanding number of suicides of hapless folks with the re-

motest connection to the president—from Vincent Foster to several down-home critics." He began:

"Q: What was O. J.'s biggest mistake?"

"A: He could have taken Nicole to Arkansas, where
she would have killed herself."

"Beirut without guns," was Tom Freidman's descrip-
tion of the Washington that Mr. Clinton came to—and
that he came to about the same time after four years as
the *New York Times'* bureau chief in Jerusalem. "The politics of moral annihilation," wrote E. J. Dionne Jr. of the
Washington Post. "It's no longer enough to simply defeat,
outargue or outpoll your political opponent. In this new
approach to politics, the only test of victory is whether
an adversary's moral standing is thoroughly shredded
and destroyed. A foe cannot simply be mistaken, foolish,
impractical, or wrongheaded; he or she has to be made
into the moral equivalent of Hitler, Stalin, the Marquis de
Sade or Al Capone."

"A city of scalpels," said John Emerson, a California
lawyer screening the thousands of Democrats from
around the country who had been waiting twelve power-
hungry years for jobs high and low in a new administration. He described a typical reference this way: "I think
she's great, just great. It was a pleasure working with
her. I know people say she's not all that smart, but she
can make up for that by . . . "

It can be a hateful place. But it is a city always ready to
be conquered and pillaged, comfortable in servitude,

quick to wear bearskins if Attila breaches the Beltway. But Bill Clinton never got the capital city's practiced kow-tow, or he was too ignorant to demand it as his right after winning the battle of 1992. He was met instead by an amazing array of enemies, legions waiting to be the second to kick him on the way down. Many Republicans counted Clinton's 43 percent mandate (the same percentage President Nixon won in 1968) as not quite legitimate. That was the line pushed on the conservative radio shows that cover the country like threatening clouds. One of the more popular political talk-show hosts in Washington was, amazingly, G. Gordon Liddy Jr., the former agent of both the Federal Bureau of Investigation and Central Intelligence Agency sentenced to federal prison for conspiracy and burglary in the Watergate scandal of the 1970s. "Radio Free America" is his vehicle now, and he jokes on the air about using cut-outs of the president and Mrs. Clinton as targets for pistol practice.

Liddy may be nuts—or pretending to be. But both Republican officeholders and professional military men were heard to say that this president was not "my" president or "our" commander in chief.

Like Nixon, Clinton was capable of bringing out the worst in people, and like Nixon, people had few illusions about Clinton's "character"—most Americans, after all, met him on *60 Minutes* defending himself against adultery charges. Many ignored that and hired him for his expected competence on certain issues, particularly the

economy in a time of slow growth and 7.7 percent unemployment and the "gridlock" of federal government.
Unemployment went down under President Clinton, and
one of the places where the improvement was most dramatic was in southern Texas, where local economies
along the Mexican border boomed after the passage of
the North American Free Trade Agreement. By the end
of the second year of his administration, the president
who pushed NAFTA through had an approval rate in
that part of the country of 7 percent in private polls taken
before the midterm elections. Gallup polls taken at the
same time asked respondents to rate the president on a
scale of –5 to +5, and more than 17 percent of the respondents chose the –5. At the same time, in a *U. S.
News and World Report* poll, 20 percent of respondents
said they "hated" the president and another 25 percent
said they merely "disliked" him. The group that hated
him most were white males; the farther south they lived,
the worse the numbers for Clinton.

Why? The '60s! It's the 1960s they hate. The passion
of the people who hated what was happening then does
not seem to have diminished—and they have come to
power in Congress and in the press, too. Deep in the National Archives in Suitland, Maryland, there is a reveal-
ing memo from President Nixon to his chief of staff
H. R. Haldeman and to one of his speechwriters, a young
man named Pat Buchanan, who would one day become
a candidate for president himself. Nixon's notes were

scribbled on a *Wall Street Journal* editorial of January 12, 1970 titled: "Assaulting the Aristocracy." The subject was Vice President Spiro Agnew's attacks on what the Journal called, "the highbrows, the intellectual-beautiful- people-Eastern-liberal elite."

"Very perceptive," wrote Nixon. He underlined this passage: "The heart of the Agnew phenomenon is precisely that a class has sprung up that considers itself uniquely qualified ('the thinking people'), and is quite willing to dismiss the ordinary American with utter contempt ('the rednecks'). Mr. Agnew has merely supplied a focus for the inevitable reaction to this arrogance."

The editorial itself was as angry as the words on the side of the black bus circling Washington: "Whose theology culminates in the death of God? Whose artistic advice culminates in pornography? Whose moral advice culminates in 'anything goes' with sex and drugs? Whose children sack the universities?" Across the bottom, President Nixon wrote: "Excellent. See if we can get the editorial writer (possibly a young staffer) for our staff."

(The editorial writer, Robert Bartley, turned them down, but like Buchanan, he became a major figure as editorial page editor of the *Journal* in the ongoing conservative struggle to repeal the 1960s.)

Then along came Clinton, arguing that he and his credentialed crew from the Ivy League and Oxford were indeed uniquely qualified to run Arkansas and then all the United States. Next to him was his credentialed and uppity wife. "Bitches like her" is an unpleasant and angry phrase hard to escape whenever Hillary Rodham Clinton is in the news. And the hatred is not because of the great events of his presidency, such as they are, but because of the great events of the recent past, particularly the 1960s—the anti-authoritarianism, the undigested revolutions, the attacks on great institutions from government to education to religion, the overthrow of patriotism and traditional American history. Bill and Hillary Clinton, the president and first lady, symbolize the 1960s to many Americans; they symbolize civil rights and feminism, sexual tolerance and abortion. For a lot of people that's when America went wrong. And the Clintons were right there.

8.
Prolonged Adolescence

Beyond the prolonged adolescence common in politicians, there may be something of a resistance to both authority and exercising it in the Clinton generation and the Clinton administration—starting at the top.

There seems to be something like a computer virus hidden in the generation that produced Bill Clinton. The 1960s people seem ridden by self-distrust, a lack of confidence in themselves and their peers—generational suspicion and jealousy of each other, some of it related to who served, who dodged, and who protested during the Vietnam years. "What do you think of 'our' President?" David Letterman asked Stevie Nicks of Fleetwood Mac, whose 1977 song "Don't Stop Thinking About Tomorrow" was the Clinton campaign's theme.

"He's too young to be president," she said. "He's my age."

The two icons of baby-boomdom—Letterman, too, is the same age—looked at each other a little strangely and moved on to funnier things.

In *Newsweek,* columnist Joe Klein, another peer of the

President, wondered whether anyone of his generation deserved to govern because their common life experience was so thin compared with the generations that survived the Great Depression and World War II. Secretary of Labor Robert Reich, who was a Rhodes Scholar with Clinton at Oxford, put it this way: "The process of decision-making [here] is very different from the process of decision-making of the generation that went before us. . . . The revolts of the '60s were very much in reaction to the hierarchical society we inherited. . . . I've decided a lot of it is deliberate, not just at the White House, but in my own department as well. I'm much more comfortable making decisions sitting around a table with assistants than sitting at a desk checking a box."*

I asked Clinton about that, about how much of the anti-authoritarianism of his 1960s he still carries with him. "Quite a bit," he answered. "I mean I share a lot of this sort of populist skepticism about Washington, which is one of the things that is frustrating to me when I identify

* Hearing that argument, Chase Untermeyer, an Assistant Secretary of the Navy under President Reagan and then personnel director of the Bush White House, suggested that there were significant differences between Democratic and Republican (or liberal and conservative) baby boomers—or perhaps between those who opposed and those who supported the war in Vietnam. Young men and women on the right, he said, fit readily and traditionally into political and governmental leadership positions. He cited Governors William Weld of Massachusetts, John Engler of Michigan, George W. Bush of Texas, and Federal officials Paul Wolfowitz, Richard Haass, John Lehman, and Robert Kimmitt.

with it, just because I can't cut through the fog that often surrounds us now and touch the American people."

That must make it tough to play the great authority figure. However that affects him, Clinton does seem ambivalent about using the power of his office. Certainly he's no father-figure of his country. When he spoke before the French National Assembly in June of 1994, he walked through a member's library with walls hung with Delacroix's bravura paintings. "Wow!" said the president of the United States. "This is terrific!"

Speak first, think later. The president was at the *Boston Globe* trying to sell his wife's universal health care plan in the summer of 1994 and he said that maybe "universal" could be 95 percent, rather than the 100 percent she was pushing. As the words came out, Clinton shook his head and looked over at Thomas Oliphant, a *Globe* columnist who traveled with him during the 1992 campaign, and whispered, "Godammit! I blew it."

An editor who overheard came up to Oliphant later and said: "He's like a big kid."

9.
The Kids in the White House

General Colin Powell, then chairman of the Joint Chiefs of Staff, tells this story about the Clinton White House: "He was . . . surrounded by young civilians without a shred of military experience or understanding. One day, my assistant, Lieutenant General Barry McCaffrey, went to the White House for a meeting. Walking through the West Wing, McCaffrey passed a young White House staffer and said, 'Hello, there,' to which she replied with upturned nose, 'We don't talk to soldiers around here.'"

Clinton, who was in Seattle for a trade meeting, heard about the snub, probably from Powell, and General Mc-Caffrey was next seen jogging along Puget Sound with the president—to calm down the Pentagon.

There are a million stories about the kids in this White House. The phrase itself, "The kids in the White House"—is perjorative, a symbol of many things Washington finds threatening, particularly outsiders and the disorder of disorganization. News of their doings was chattered about by the hard-core Beltway Democrats, the middle-level officials President Jimmy Carter had left behind in the last Democratic retreat, who survived as lobbyists and demi-journalists after 1980. A high official from those olden days of the 1970s, recruited into the Clinton administration in what seemed a constant Clinton search for a man with the key to the city—Gergen, Cutler, Panetta—reported back to Georgetown, in shock, that the kids did not stand up when the president entered a room. Some of them left their feet on the table, he said, as the president talked—and talked. Like graduate students.

Then, in 1995, Washington was rattled by another youth-quake, the arrival of the young, zealous and restless freshmen (and women) of the 104th Congress. They flaunted their hatred of Washington and almost everyone there—some literally refused to speak to Democratic members during their first months in town.

The White House kids didn't talk to outsiders either, working all hours and pretty much ignoring anyone who was not in the Clinton campaign before them, speaking only to each other, sleeping on couches. Stories abounded, most of them true, of hours of bull sessions in the White House, issue-of-the-day seminars with more and more passersby joining the fun, which was often presided over by the biggest kid of them all, Bill Clinton.

Because of them—or the perception of them—a new category of Washington player was conversationally created, "The Grown-ups." The godfather of that group was

Secretary of the Treasury Lloyd Bentsen and included Gergen, Cutler, and Pannetta and Democrats like Senators Sam Nunn of Georgia and Bill Bradley of New Jersey.

In fact, though, the White House kids were not all as young as they seemed. The presidency has always depended on the undivided energy of young assistants. Their symbol now is Stephanopoulos, who was thirty-one when he came to the White House, the same age Theodore Sorensen was when he came to the White House with Kennedy, three years older than Bill Moyers when he joined Lyndon Johnson's White House in 1963. But the times have changed and so have young lifestyles—Sorensen and Moyers were really young old men, with suits and ties, wives, children, and mortgages. Also, they did not put their feet up or wear earrings— and they returned phone calls.

The kids and the calls are a recurring complaint. When we talked in late 1993, the president's complaint was that the most important newspapers, particularly the *New York Times* and the *Washington Post,* were killing him by turning one-day stories into two-day front-page stories. He said they were reporting on possible administration decisions or moves on one day, without White House comment or explanation, and then running the comment, often a denial, the next day. That sounded about right to me, but when I mentioned it to reporters covering the administration, I got a string of laughing or growling answers like this from Al Kamen, a *Washington Post* columnist: "Tell Clinton that we'd be glad to print what he has to say if those kids over there would return calls before deadline instead of after 8 o'clock or not at all."

An important Democratic member of Congress put it this way: "There's no one to talk to down there, they're at meetings all day."

The Clinton folk also give lousy tape. Because it took so long to get any kind of call-back from the president's pollster, Stanley Greenberg, who should know better at the age of fifty-two, I was able to memorize this message:

"You have reached Greenberg Research. You may leave a message for Stan or Chris by pushing one. Joe, two. Benita and Robert, three. Al or his assistant, Dana, four. Kathy or Alan, five. Dane and Derek, six. John, Vickie, or Bruce, seven. Nicole, eight. Margaret or main reception, nine."

The man at the center of all this, President Clinton, once said of himself: "I acted forty when I was sixteen, and I acted sixteen when I was forty." That would make him twenty-four now. This is from John Brummett, a columnist for the *Arkansas Democrat-Gazette* on the politician he had followed for fifteen years: "An insecure overgrown boy, who seems to lack grounding or certainty about who or what he is."

Perhaps because he is so intelligent, Clinton does not have a "Go/No Go" mind of the type that serves many military men and political leaders so well. In fact, he often sounds like an encyclopedia without an index. He is not, by any measure, wise beyond his years, possibly because he has had such limited life experience—school and politics, that's about it. He was never in the armed services or the Peace Corps; he's never really held a job in the private sector. "If I lose, do you think I could make one hundred thousand dollars a year?" he asked a friend, Will Marshall, president of the Progressive Policy Institute. "That would be good, wouldn't it? Could I make that?"

Like a kid, he does seem to instinctively avoid responsibility and blame and personal confrontation, too—psychohistorians have fun with that, leaping immediately to possibilities of childhood abuse—usually talking about how hard he works and how he tries to do too much all at once.

Margaret G. Hermann, a professor of political science at Ohio State and author of two books on the psychology of political leaders, has tried to catalog the elements of what she calls "The Clinton Factor," coming up with a shortlist that could describe many graduate students— or teenagers: "His perpetual lateness . . . his quick temper . . . his talking to the very last person at an event . . . his complaining about lack of free time when all those he invited actually drop by . . . his limitless energy . . . his love of politics, cajoling, log-rolling, and trench fighting that make up consensus building . . . his desire to be in the center of everything . . . his perserverance and dedication . . . his thriving on chaos and uncertainty."

"Thriving on chaos" is one of Clinton's true links to the president of his youth, John F. Kennedy, the man he says inspired his life in politics. (I tend to think young Bill Clinton had begun running for president long before the day he shook Kennedy's hand on the White House lawn in July of 1963.) Like Kennedy, Clinton describes his running of the White House as being at the center of a wheel, as opposed to presidents like Dwight Eisenhower and Ronald Reagan, whose organizational styles were top-down structures, like a military or corporate organization chart or a classic pyramid. There is a fundamental difference between men who run things from the top and those who want to be at the center of the action. It's lonely at the top and Clinton does not like being alone. That is, alas, a political character trait that more often than not makes the best candidates the worst executives or administrators because that work has to be done at a desk—alone.

Well into Clinton's second year as president, Ann Devroy of the *Washington Post* wrote of the White House she covered under the headline: "Loops of Power Snarl in Clinton White House—Mistakes and Confusion Seem to be a Way of Life." The story below included these phrases: "Wild ride . . . breathtaking lurches . . . constantly reinventing itself . . . new people learning their jobs . . . blissful ignorance . . . lines of authority resemble a plate of spaghetti."

Men like Clinton (and Kennedy) are addicted to action. For restless, impatient, excitement-driven politicians, life can be a race against boredom, and confusion is power, a way of controlling other people by keeping them off-balance. The president may need a disciplined and organized chief of staff (and wife), but when the new chief of staff, Leon Panetta, tried to move out thirty-two-year-old press secretary Dee Dee Myers, she was able to run puffy-eyed to the president and win a reprieve— and remind everyone, including Panetta, who really makes the decisions. The White House Panetta came to was, to say the least, a bit unsettled. On his fifth day on the job, July 22, 1994, these are the headlines Panetta read coming off the Dow Jones newswire in one minute, between 3:08 P.M. and 3:09 P.M.: "Panetta: Clinton Has 'Full Confidence' in Fgn. Policy Team" . . . "Panetta Says Clinton Has Confidence in HUD Secy. Cisneros" . . . "Panetta Says Clinton Has 'Confidence' in Agric. Secy. Espy."

So I was surprised, as the president and I talked about my book, *President Kennedy: Profile of Power,* when he said he was fascinated reading of the disorganization in the Kennedy White House and that he sure was glad that he had no problems like that. He mentioned a May 1961 memo from Kennedy's National Security Adviser, McGeorge Bundy, to the president, saying: "I hope you'll be in a good mood when you read this. . . . We do have a problem of management; centrally it is a problem of your use of time. We can't get you to sit still. . . . The National

Security Council, for example, really cannot work for you unless you authorize work schedules that do not get upset from day to day. Calling three meetings in five days is foolish—and putting them off for six weeks at a time is just as bad. . . . A couple of weeks ago, you asked me to begin to meet you (regularly in the morning). I have succeeded in catching you on three mornings, for a total of about eight minutes. Moreover, six of the eight minutes were an exercise in who leaked and why . . . "

In October and November of 1993, Secretary of State Warren Christopher, Defense Secretary Les Aspin, and NSC chief Lake got together to send Clinton a series of memos pleading with the president to give them one hour a week to discuss international affairs. Clinton finally said, "Yes," scrawling at the bottom of the last memo, "When possible." It turned out it was possible only once, on November 12—after that, as before, briefings came only with crises.

So perhaps nothing is ever totally new at the White House. Roosevelt was the man there when Will Rogers wrote in his daily column in 1934: "They are just children that's never grown up. . . . Keep off the radio till you've got something to say. . . . Stay off that back lawn with those photographers. Nothing will kill interest in a president quicker."

10.
HRC: The First Lady

One of the stories Les Aspin took away from the White House after his year as secretary of defense involved a policy called "lift and strike" in the civil war in Bosnia and the rest of what was once Yugoslavia. The idea was that the United States and other Western governments could save the struggling government of Bosnia (mostly Muslim) and end the Bosnian Serb (Christian) siege of the capital city of Sarajevo by: (1) lifting the U. S.-enforced arms embargo on Bosnian Muslims, giving them the weapons to defend themselves against Bosnian Serbs; and (2) striking Bosnian Serb positions using the warplanes of NATO (the North Atlantic Treaty Organization), the U. S.-dominated European military alliance.

While Secretary of State Warren Christopher was in Europe informing NATO member governments of Clinton's decision to back "lift and strike," Aspin went to the White House on a Monday morning for a routine ceremony. The president came downstairs holding a book, *Balkan Ghosts* by Robert Kaplan, a history of centuries of war in that part of the world. He said his wife had read it over the weekend and he had looked at it, too. The message the Clintons took from the book was that these people had been killing each other for ten centuries past and probably would do the same for centuries.

"Holy shit!" Aspin remembered thinking that morning. "He's going south on 'lift and strike'."

And he did. It was not the first time nor the last that a Clinton decision made downstairs was reversed when he went upstairs. Whatever happens in what she calls her "zone of privacy," Mrs. Clinton is the final adviser to the president. She is what Robert Kennedy was to his brother and then some. She is the last loyalist, the only one with no other political agenda than the rise of Bill Clinton.

Bill Clinton married Hillary Rodham because he thought she was the smartest girl he ever met. He believes he would not have become president without her. He's probably right about both things, certainly the second one.

There are those of us who think that there should be no such thing as the title "First Lady." She should have the "zone of privacy" she talks about, one a lot bigger than she has now—by staying away from public business as long as she is not held as accountable as any ordinary unrelated federal official. She has never been elected to anything and you do not have to be a sworn political opponent of the Clintons to be uneasy about the idea of secret power at the highest levels without any public accountability. Unlike every other person around the president, she cannot be fired, ignored, impeached, or defeated in election.

Having said that, I think this first lady is a serious, intelligent, disciplined woman, feminine, more vain than stylish, obviously a good and caring mother, a true believer in the family values that many Americans mouth for those who prefer hearing about them to living with them. She is an altogether admirable individual by most any measure.

My wife and I were in the White House in October of 1993 because the president had been reading my book on President Kennedy. After a few minutes, Mrs. Clinton came into the Oval Office. I said that it was a pleasure to meet her because I admired what she was trying to do on health care and other things. (I spared her my opinion that first ladies should be seen more than heard.)

"Actually," she said, "we've met before,"—and she reminded me of things we had talked about in the past. We all chatted for a few minutes and I asked the president if he could show me the direction the British had come from during the War of 1812 when they set fire to the White House—and, it is said, the first lady, Dolley Madison, saved the originals of the Declaration of Indepen-

dence and the Constitution. He could and we walked outside for a couple of minutes. When we came back in,
Mrs. Clinton said: "I hope you don't think I'm too so-
cially forward, but I've got a hungry president on my
hands. Are you guys free for lunch?"

We allowed that we might be able to make the time.
We talked for a couple of hours in the small walled garden just outside the president's small hideaway office,
ironically, a very European setting. Much of the conversation was about the differences in being president
when the nation was united in determination to win the
Cold War. "I envy Kennedy having an enemy," Clinton
said, thinking it must have been a good deal easier to
sell programs and ideas negatively, just by shouting that
the Russians were coming. "The question now, is how to
persuade people they should do things when they are
not immediately threatened," he said. "Believe me it's
harder to do it positively." He said, too, that he was
greatly impressed with Kennedy's ability to hold decisions open for as long as possible without constantly
being called indecisive.

"How did he do that?" he asked. The answer was that
Kennedy did not analyze and agonize over decisions in
public and his men knew what would happen to them if
they ever leaked stories of his private indecision. That is
what I should have said, but I was more indirect, not having the courage to tell my president in person that he

talked too much. Things like that are easier from behind a typewriter.

After he said there was no disorganization in his White House, we went on to the almost exponential growth in the size of the presidency and the difficulty of sorting out the people who want to feed their passion for distinction by presidential appointment. When Ted Sorensen was White House counsel, I said, that was essentially a person, not a department. Now the White House has dozens of in-house attorneys—it is a scale model of the Justice Department—many, if not most of them, working on security checks of potential appointees. They have to be sure Clinton appoints no Communists or, worse, women with undocumented nannies. At the rate they are working, this president will not be able to fill all the judgeships and other appointments he is empowered to make by the end of his term in January of 1997. Again, more than a thousand people in the White House can say "No," but we were sitting with the only two who could say "Yes."

Mrs. Clinton was the perfect hostess that afternoon as her husband did most of the talking—and the perfect political wife, too, listening as if she had never heard such wisdom before in her life. Only once did there seem to be tension between them. The steward came out with the dessert menus and the president kept sneaking looks over at his wife. When she didn't return the glances, he said softly: "Maybe I'll try the blueberry pie? Just a little." Finally, after an hour or so, Mrs. Clinton excused herself, saying, "I have work to do."

The *New York Times* was undoubtedly right, too, when it concluded Hillary Rodham Clinton was "pretending" when she tried to play a nice Pillsbury Bake-Off lady during the 1992 campaign. Perhaps she played at being a homebody, but she is not pretending as wife and mother. What she is pretending to be is a politician—as opposed to an engaged and energetic citizen. Her husband, even at his worst, has political instincts if not convictions. She has convictions, but the political instincts of a stone. "It is a fundamental problem in the Clintons' White House," said one of the president's men, emphasizing the "s" in Clintons. "She ain't got rhythm!"

Her people, the ones she brought into the White House, have mostly failed, beginning with the Clinton's first counsel, Bernard Nussbaum, her mentor when she was a junior attorney on the staff of the House Judiciary Committee during the Watergate investigation in 1974. And so have her pals from the Rose Law Firm, beginning with Wade Hubbell, who was forced to resign as associate attorney general and pleaded guilty to criminal fraud charges on Rose billings and expense accounts. Nussbaum's deputy, a former Rose partner, Vincent Foster, committed suicide on July 20, 1993, leaving a torn-up note that said: "I made mistakes from ignorance, inexperience and overwork . . . I was not meant for the job or the spotlight of public life in Washington. Here ruining people is considered sport."

Quite naturally, Mrs. Clinton is greatly resented by most of the president's staff—some hate her, more try to avoid her—because they find her a cold and arrogant judge of their best efforts and because of her effect on her husband's moods. More than a few of them dread the weekends the Clintons spend together at Camp David, leery of the arrogance and petty paranoia the two of them can feed in each other—what was called "bunker mentality" when she was working on Watergate. Except for Hillary and Gore, Clinton does not have a notable record of seeking out challenging contemporaries. No grown-ups, some would say—and do. The FOBs—Friends of Bill—are something of a myth. He knows hundreds or thousands of people, but the folks who make it to the White House or Camp David or Martha's Vineyard are interesting strangers. On the Vineyard, a woman asked what was the best thing about being president and he answered: "I can meet anyone I want to—and visit with them."

Hillary Clinton is the only constant in his life, the best friend. Some of the bright young men of a new generation around Clinton, the kids, have seen too much of the president as a hostage to his wife—turning his palms up, shrugging slightly in a "What can I do?" gesture when the subject turned to health care or Whitewater. Some see her as part of him, an unpredictable part of his mood and mind—more powerful in that way than Bobby Kennedy ever was. President Kennedy never came down the elevator from the family quarters in a rage or depressed because of arguments with his brother as Clinton did for weeks at the end of 1993, yelling and sulking, distracted downstairs by what was happening between himself and his wife upstairs.

11.
Sex and the
Clinton Collapse

Bill Clinton had taken an emotional dive in the late spring of 1993, losing confidence in himself in the "Incredible Shrinking President" period when everything seemed to be going wrong—and working harder and later did not help. But he snapped out of it pretty quickly, partly because the press was distracted and got off his back after the surprising appointment of David Gergen as his designated leaker. It does not usually take much to make reporters happy, and Gergen knew how to do it.

It was much worse at the end of that year—even after the president's run of real successes with the Democratic Congress. Gergen was already in terminal decline, victim of a thousand cuts from the White House kids whittling him down to size, outnumbering and outleaking him. Worse than that, he had unknowingly crossed Mrs. Clinton by repeatedly urging the president to try to slosh out of the quagmire of Whitewater by releasing everything, bank statements, contracts, whatever documents they had, to press and public. How bad could it be? Clinton, according to Gergen's reasoning, saw money primarily as fuel for campaigns. The Clintons did not want to own the country, they just wanted to run it. True enough, but Hillary Clinton ran the family finances and as far as she was concerned that was not anybody else's business—David Gergen was anybody else.

The family crisis at the end of the year was not about money, though. It was set off by a new wave of stories and speculation about Clinton's wandering sexual ways back in Arkansas, particularly a nasty piece titled "Living With The Clintons" by a writer named David Brock in *The American Spectator,* a conservative journal that also happens to be helped along by money from the foundations of Richard Mellon Scaife. The article was based mainly on interviews with four Arkansas state troopers (two identified, two anonymous) who had served as Governor Clinton's bodyguards and drivers. It went on for eleven thousand words about everything from oral sex in pickup trucks with department store clerks to the dropping of gubernatorial pants before a state employee identified only as "Paula." (The last name turned out to be "Jones," and soon she was holding press conferences and filing lawsuits demanding a presidential apology.)

Hillary Clinton was devastated. She took it out on her husband and, in a way, he took it out on the country, beginning with his own staff.

Much of the Brock piece was sleaze of a not particularly high order, allegations, rumors, supposition—"as has been widely rumored" was considered sourcing in published footnotes—and staffers had tried to keep the magazine away from the Clintons. They hoped, vainly, that the "mainstream press" might not pick up the story. Forget that in Prigogine's exploding and imploding Washington. The *Los Angeles Times* weighed in with four thousand better-documented words on the same troopers— the story Representative Dornan previewed on Rush Limbaugh's show—and the cops from Little Rock were on television within hours.

Then, on the Sunday before Christmas, the *New York Times* reported that Vincent Foster's papers had apparently included a Whitewater file, which had never been listed on the White House inventory of documents found in his office. At the White House staff Christmas party, the Clintons left after only five minutes. They were barely looking at each other.

The momentum of the old year was quickly lost. On January 9, 1994, Senator Daniel Patrick Moynihan of New York, the chairman of the Senate Finance Committee, appeared on NBC's *Meet the Press*—moderated again by Tim Russert, his former press secretary—and called for a special prosecutor for Whitewater and then began the torpedoing of the Clinton's health care plans. "We don't have a health care crisis in this country," he said. "We do have a welfare crisis."

Moynihan had been making that argument in private for some time—put welfare reform first because there is a consensus among both Republicans and Democrats for change—and so had many other elected officials. But that could not be done unless Hillary Clinton agreed to close down the health care deliberations that led to a thirteen-thousand-page summary and recommendations— and she most decidedly did not agree.

The idea that such grand-scale change in American life, arrived at in secret meetings of "experts," could be pushed whole through Congress or past the American people without debate, amendment, or consensus offended thinking politicians. One of them said: "Great enterprises should not be built on small majorities"—that from Thomas Jefferson. The third president could have added "Or on minorities." The thirty-fifth president, Kennedy, who like Clinton won with less than 50 percent of the total vote, carried a slip of paper around with a number on it—118,574—to remind himself of his tiny majority of votes over Nixon in the 1960 election. Clinton, for all his political brilliance, often seemed numb to the fact that though he won a plurality in 1992's three-man field, 57 percent of his countrymen voted against him and most of them were probably inclined to do it again if they got the chance.

For Moynihan, who had come to Washington first as a kid of his time, a thirty-four-year-old assistant in the Kennedy White House, it was time to pay back the newest generation of kids in the White House. The New York senator had been dismissed by the new breed, one of whom (he believed it was Stephanopoulos) was quoted in *Time* magazine as saying during the transition: "He's not one of us. . . . He's cantankerous, but he couldn't obstruct us even if he wanted to. We'll roll right over him if we have to."

Nine days later, Bobby Ray Inman, a former deputy CIA director nominated by Clinton to succeed Les Aspin as secretary of defense, called a press conference in Austin, Texas. His performance was the stuff of legend or Oliver Stone films, one of the screwball screw-ups of all time. Inman said he did not want the job because there was a conspiracy of reporters and Republican senators trying to destroy him. Then on January 20, the first anniversary of Clinton's inaugural, Attorney General Janet Reno appointed a special prosecutor to investigate the charges collected under the headline "Whitewater." On the Larry King show that night, the president said: "It was a little tougher to change things than I thought it would be. . . . But everybody here gets up and goes to work every day and works like crazy."

After that, for a year, no matter how hard he worked, almost everything that could go wrong for President Clinton did go wrong, climaxing in the election of the angry and conservative 104th Congress. But through 1995 he turned it around again, sounding like a Republican himself as the torrential momentum of the new Congress faded into over-confidence, bickering, fatigue and the trickles of presidential politics of real Republicans beginning with Senator Dole and Speaker Gingrich. By the end of the year, the Republican tough guys learned what the press already knew: Beating up Bill Clinton is something like punching a pillow.

But then the other Clinton became the target, a more brittle one. As 1996 began, congressional Republicans managed to force the disclosure of White House memos and old Rose Law Firm records that showed Hillary Rodham Clinton had more to do with the little scandals of Whitewater and the firing of White House travel office employees than she or her friends and assistants had admitted—even under oath before Congress. As Mrs. Clinton's staff and protectors repeatedly avoided or evaded linking her to missing records and such, one woman who worked with but not for the first lady said bitterly: "Just another couple of people whose lives will be ruined by misplaced loyalty to Hillary Clinton."

A presidency, too, could be ruined by the tangled webs of loyalty and betrayal, gratitude and anger between Bill and Hillary Clinton.

12.
Somebody up There Doesn't Like Me

My interview with President Clinton at the end of 1994 began on time. With Clinton that was news. Periodically, which means when things look bad, he gives himself over to handlers, staff members who try to get him out of rooms or towns before he says too much, too soon.

A year earlier in the White House, we had begun late, but a scheduled ten-minute drop-by with my wife on October 10, 1993, had stretched into two hours of lunch and conversation. The talk then, most of it by him, had been interrupted only by three polite attempts to break it up by George Stephanopoulos, standing silently until the president looked his way and then whispering that the minority leader of the Senate, Bob Dole, was on the telephone hoping to talk about Haiti and application of the War Powers Act requiring notice to Congress of military actions. The day before, a Navy ship, the USS *Harlan County,* attempting to land American and Canadian military police at Port Au Prince, had sailed back home on the president's orders rather than confront a few dozen thugs yelling the local equivalent of "Yankee Go Home!" The leader of the demonstrators, it turned out, was on the payroll of the Central Intelligence Agency.

The President ignored Stephanapoulos—and Dole—and talked on.

This time, though, on October 18, 1994, the interview was different. Stephanopoulos and another assistant, Mark Gearan, were sitting on a couch in the president's office, placed so that he could see them but I could not. A couple of times, when I bent over my notes, Clinton looked over to his men, apparently seeking acknowledgment that he was "on message," that he was "sticking to his script for the day." He was paying attention, being good. Halfway through the interview, he repeated something he had said before: "Like I said, you know, before you started taking notes, 'If I were a Republican . . . '"

Then, after a half-hour or so, Leon Panetta came in, an obvious signal that it was time to end this. I was asking, "Why do so many people dislike you so much . . . ?"

"The radical right and the Congressional Republicans have demonized me," he answered. "Like I said, if they had a president who'd done what I'd done . . . "

Then he slipped the bonds of office for a moment, stood up, bent over me, and said:

"You know the story about the guy who falls off the mountain, and he's falling down into the canyon to certain death? . . . And he sees this little twig coming out of the mountain and he grabs it as a last-ditch thing. He's holding on, and the roots start coming out of the mountain, and he looks down at hundreds of feet below, and he says: 'God, why me?'

"'I'm a good man, I work hard, I follow the law. Why me?' And this thunderous voice comes out of the heavens and says: 'Son, there's just something about you I don't like!'"

"Do you know what that something is?" I asked.

"No," Clinton said. "All I know is that I work hard at this job. I try to do what's best for mainstream American people . . . "